"Lauren Crews delivers a powerful message amazing ability to balance teaching through the Hebrew acrostic and sharing relevant and vulnerable stories that tug at the heart. I've read Proverbs 31 too many times to count, but Lauren brought it alive in a brand-new, thought-provoking way. This is not a book to be missed!"

—Bethany Jett, award-winning author
of *Platinum Faith* and *They Call Me Mom*

"*Strength of a Woman* is an answer to prayer for every woman who has ever resented the Proverbs 31 Woman as it reveals this passage of Scripture actually celebrates our worth, value, and strength as women. We no longer need to feel inferior to the woman showcased in Proverbs 31; instead, we can celebrate her because we are her . . . or at least we have the opportunity to be. While this isn't a quick read, its contents are worth every minute spent immersed in the Hebraic insights this author brings out in a very relatable manner. Get *Strength of a Woman* and grow stronger in your walk with God."

—Michelle Medlock Adams, award-winning and best-selling author
of more than ninety books, including *Platinum Faith*,
They Call Me Mom, and *Fabulous and Focused*

"Author Lauren Crews has given us a great gift by writing *Strength of a Woman*, allowing us the opportunity to reconnect with the Proverbs 31 Woman—not as an unrealistic goal or proof of failure—but as an attainable model for a strong woman of God."

—Edie Melson, award-winning author
and director of the Blue Ridge Mountains Christian Writers Conference

"In *Strength of a Woman*, Lauren Crews dives into the secrets revealed in the Hebrew language and contemplates the famous virtuous woman's passage in Proverbs 31. Lauren explains the passage was not designed to make women feel overwhelmed by an impossible to-do list but rather serves to promote the warrior woman you can emulate as you love, work, build, and overcome your own life's challenges. A great read!"

—Linda Evans Shepherd, author of *When You Need to Move a Mountain*,
publisher of *Leading Hearts* magazine and Arise Daily Devotionals,
founder of the Advanced Writers and Speakers Association

"I believe we've lost much of the meaning of Scripture by not incorporating our Jewish roots and the Hebrew language. I'm a Bible nerd, and I often incorporate Hebrew in my own writing, but Lauren Crews takes us one more step by introducing the symbolism of the Hebrew alphabet. What could have been painfully academic, Lauren has gracefully written in a way that relates to our hearts. *Strength of a Woman* gently and beautifully teaches us about the true and empowering meaning of Proverbs 31. If you've tried to measure up to this 'perfect' wife and mother, this is a must-read."

—Andy Lee, author of *A Mary Like Me: Flawed Yet Called*

"I've always called the Proverbs 31 Woman, 'The Intimidating Mrs. P-31.' She is seemingly depicted as 'all that and a bag of chips'—an unattainable standard of womanhood that leaves the rest of us feeling less-than. In *Strength of a Woman*, author Lauren Crews sheds new and insightful biblical light on the woman who has intimidated many women throughout the ages. Using the Hebraic symbolism of the Jewish language and stories from modern-day real life Proverbs 31 women, Lauren's unique approach gives readers a deeper understanding of this often misunderstood but power-packed passage of Scripture. With discussion questions and prayer prompts in every chapter, *Strength of a Woman* is a great resource for individuals and groups alike. I highly recommend it."

—Stephanie Shott, Bible teacher, author, and founder of The MOM Initiative

"In her beautiful book, Lauren paints a masterpiece from the canvas of Scripture by utilizing Hebrew poetry, word pictures, and personal stories to bring the *Strength of a Woman* to life. Her colors and shading through acrostic poetry and the Hebrew alphabet focus on the attributes of the Proverbs 31 Woman and the character of Jesus Christ with spiritual introspection throughout. This magnum opus will transform your understanding of God through the beauty of His language."

—Debbie Blank, president, Living Word Ministries

LAUREN CREWS

Strength
of a
Woman

WHY YOU ARE PROVERBS 31

ASCENDER
BOOKS
An Imprint of Iron Stream Media
BIRMINGHAM, ALABAMA

Ascender Books
100 Missionary Ridge
Birmingham, AL 35242
Ascender Books is an imprint of Iron Stream Media
IronStreamMedia.com

Iron Stream Media serves its authors as they express their views, which may not express the views
of the publisher.

Library of Congress Cataloging-in-Publication Data

Names: Crews, Lauren, 1967- author.
Title: Strength of a woman : why you are Proverbs 31 / Lauren Crews.
Description: First. | Birmingham, Alabama : Ascender Books, an imprint of
    Iron Stream Media, 2020.
Identifiers: LCCN 2019051310 (print) | LCCN 2019051311 (ebook) | ISBN
    9781563093371 | ISBN 9781563093425 (ebook)
Subjects: LCSH: Bible. Proverbs, XXXI—Criticism, interpretation, etc. |
    Women—Biblical teaching.
Classification: LCC BS1465.52 .C74 2020 (print) | LCC BS1465.52 (ebook) |
    DDC 248.8/43--dc23
LC record available at https://lccn.loc.gov/2019051310
LC ebook record available at https://lccn.loc.gov/2019051311

All Scripture quotations, unless otherwise indicated, are taken from the New American Standard Bible®,
Copyright © 1960, 1962, 1963, 1968, 1971, 1972, 1973, 1975, 1977, 1995 by The Lockman Foundation
Used by permission.

Scripture quotations marked (KJV) are taken from The Holy Bible, King James Version.

Scripture quotations marked (ESV) are from The Holy Bible, English Standard Version® (ESV®),
copyright © 2001 by Crossway, a publishing ministry of Good News Publishers. Used by permission.
All rights reserved.

Scripture quotations marked (NIV) are taken from the Holy Bible, New International Version®, NIV®.
Copyright © 1973, 1978, 1984, 2011 by Biblica, Inc.™ Used by permission of Zondervan. All rights
reserved worldwide. www.zondervan.com The "NIV" and "New International Version" are trademarks
registered in the United States Patent and Trademark Office by Biblica, Inc.™

Scripture quotations from THE MESSAGE. Copyright © by Eugene H. Peterson 1993, 1994, 1995, 1996,
2000, 2001, 2002. Used by permission of Tyndale House Publishers, Inc.

Author is represented by the literary agency of Credo Communications, LLC, Grand Rapids, Michigan,
www.credocommunication.net.

ISBN-13: 978-1-56309-337-1
Ebook ISBN: 978-1-56309-342-5

1 2 3 4 5—24 23 22 21 20

Dedicated to the women who allowed me to share not only the struggles and pain of their stories but also their victories and redemption. Proverbs 31 reveals your warrior strength. We can do hard things. *Eishet Chayil!*

Other books by Lauren Crews

Strength of a Woman Devotional: 31 Days to Celebrating Your Place in Proverbs 31

CONTENTS

This book began as a Tuesday night Bible study in my home with women who helped me hone the correct words and dig into provoking questions. I am so very appreciative of Terri, Melissa, Tammy, Angie, Margaret, Avery, and Lisa. They say it takes a village to raise a child. After years of work, slashing edits, crippling insecurities, major rewrites . . . and waiting . . . I feel as though I'm graduating an unruly teenager more so than giving birth.

Thank you to my village of readers, editors, and teachers who have encouraged and patiently worked with me. What began as a Holy Spirit, word-nerd nudge grew into a vision of redemption and value. I am forever grateful that the God of the universe would challenge me to be strong and courageous in following Him.

Your Heroic Hymn

I need to be honest with you from the start. From what I first learned about the Proverbs 31 Woman, I hated her. History portrayed her as a virtuous flower and upheld her as a glowing example of biblical womanhood. I saw her as a standard.

I'm not wealthy, I don't know how to weave fabric, and I'm not a stay-at-home mom. Some days I'm so busy the best I can do for dinner is the drive-through. And, honestly, sometimes it's hard to honor my husband. When you add to that the challenges other women face in divorce, as a single parent, or as a widow, or the guilt and rejection some women feel if they cannot conceive, how can we not walk away from the passage feeling judged? She is everywhere. But I. just. can't. do. it.

I took a Facebook survey of my friends and contacts asking, "What is your first thought when you hear Proverbs 31 mentioned?" Some women replied, "A godly example like my grandmother," or, "Something to strive for." However, the typical response was, "Too much, a lot to achieve." The overwhelming response was, "Unobtainable, I try but fail often"—and they felt bad for failing.

Once upon a time I too related to the Proverbs 31 Woman in this way, but I've changed my mind.

Would it surprise you to know the verses of Proverbs 31:10–31 have a military theme and emphasize strength? Throughout the passage, the verses make references to military activities and the spoils of war. Historically this passage is read as a heroic hymn. In *The Song of a Valiant Woman*, author Al Wolters says this type of literature is found in many cultures and is "characterized by the recounting of the mighty deeds of heroes, usually the military exploits of noble warriors."[1] Many examples of heroic hymns can be found throughout the Bible. Proverbs 31 also draws to mind the work of Old Testament priests, a second theme, developed through references to the material of the priestly garments and the Tabernacle. These themes are very different from the traditional homemaker and housewife I thought she represented.

I love the Word of God. The more I study it, the more I realize how much I don't know. But I've studied and learned the Bible through the English language and through the eyes of a modern, Western understanding. When we read the Bible today, we don't necessarily know how the original reader understood the lessons taught. We read with twenty-first century eyes. When translating, we must consider the original audience and the nuances of their language and culture. This is called hermeneutics, and it is crucial for accurate interpretation.

Yet most of us don't have a confident understanding of a foreign language like Hebrew or Greek. We aren't familiar with the figurative language, the idioms, wordplay, and puns. We just do not "get it" like the native speakers do, and, as a result, some of the meaning gets lost in translation.

When a friend mentioned Proverbs 31:10–31 is an acrostic poem written with the Hebrew alphabet, it stirred my word-nerd juices. I had to investigate. Hebrew is a verbal language, which means it is best understood through speaking. It was common in the Jewish culture

---

1. Al Wolters, *The Song of the Valiant Woman: Studies in the Interpretation of Proverbs 31:10–31* (Waynesboro, GA: Paternoster Press, 2001), 9.

to memorize the Torah, so much so a rabbi might mention the first few words of a passage and his disciples would be able to fully recite the rest. When we are aware of this practice and how the people of biblical times did not have the access we do to scrolls or books of the Old Testament, it is easy to see why emphasis was placed on memorization and recitation.

Acrostic poems are commonly used in the Old Testament to aid the reader in memorization. Today we also use them to help us remember information. You may have memorized the following acrostic in school to help you remember the planets.

My	M for Mercury
Very	V for Venus
Educated	E for Earth
Mother	M for Mars
Just	J for Jupiter
Served	S for Saturn
Us	U for Uranus
Nothing	N for Neptune

If you're old school, like me, the acrostic ended with Nine Pizzas, but apparently Pluto isn't considered a planet anymore. Poor Pluto.

Like this acrostic, the Hebrew alphabet letters begin each verse of Proverbs 31:10–31 to trigger a reminder for the reader to help with memorization. I became curious how the letters might relate to the verses, and I discovered some amazing lessons we can all apply to our lives as women.

First, did you know our alphabet developed from the Phoenician and Hebrew alphabet? Our written letters began as pictures and symbols that held meaning—think cave drawings. They, in turn, developed into the letters and meanings we use today.

In Hebrew, each letter not only represents a sound but also has a picture to illustrate it. The pictograph relates to a fundamental meaning linked to the letter. As the Hebrew language developed, the word pictures for the letters were combined to form words, which included the original pictorial meaning of each letter. For example, the Hebrew word for *father* is *ab* or *abba*. The Hebrew letters to spell this word are א (*alef*) and ב (*bet*). The word picture that represents *alef* is an ox, with a fundamental symbolism of first (i.e., the first letter) and strong (i.e., "strong as an ox"). *Bet*'s word picture, on the other hand, is a house, so when you combine the word picture imagery for *ab*, you can see that father means the first strength of the house.

Hebrew letters also represent numeric values. *Alef* through *yud* represents numbers one through ten. *Kaf* through *ayin* are twenty through ninety, counting by ten. *Qof* through *tav* are one hundred through nine hundred, counting by hundreds. Sometimes knowing the numeric value of the letter will add some insight, like what we just saw in the word pictures for *ab*. Because the word picture meaning, or number value, was to aid in memorization, there is often a link between it and the verse of Proverbs 31.

The intent of observing the relationship to a number or word picture is not to discover a secret Bible code in the acrostic poem. The process is used only as an observational tool to better understand the context and reasoning behind the word choice to aid in memorization. As a poem, we look at the entire passage, not just a single verse. This is important, as is acknowledging the figurative language and extended metaphors.

We can best understand the Proverbs 31 passage as a Hebrew proverb and poetic writing, which offers general life principles, not absolutes. In the Book of Proverbs, wisdom is frequently personified as Lady Wisdom. Throughout the poem of Proverbs 31:10–31, the author provides examples of wisdom in action, which are revealed from A to Z, or in Hebrew, from *alef* to *tav*. The idiom "from A to Z" describes something that has been analyzed deeply to cover all aspects of the topic. Proverbs 31 therefore provides the actions of this woman, so we can learn wisdom from her, from A to Z.

God holds women and the work of women in high regard. The fact God included a heroic poem about the various aspects of a woman's life can be received with encouragement. Women, wives, and mothers are on the front lines and are vital when it comes to nurturing the next generation of His family, the future generation of believers. My hope is that you can lay aside any hindrances you have in embracing the life of the Proverbs 31 Woman and be strengthened and encouraged from Hebraic insight that celebrates your worth, value, and strength as a woman.

Every chapter in this book aims to provide you with some background knowledge about each of the twenty-two letters of the Hebrew alphabet and explores how the word picture relates to the verse so we might glean the Hebrew insights that add a richer layer of understanding to the writing. Sometimes the meanings and pictographs will offer a word play we would otherwise miss. Other times they will provide a deeper definition of a word, verse, or theme. I've also included the stories of uncommon Proverbs 31 Women. My prayer is that their stories will inspire you to know the source of their strength and fall more in love with Jesus Christ and the grace He alone offers.

Finally, let's discover how the word pictures of Proverbs 31 relate to women today, in all our roles of life, and how we can respond. I firmly believe these verses apply to all women in a much deeper way than just as an unattainable to-do list or a list of how to be the perfect wife. How does it apply to a divorced woman, the widow, the single mom? I offer to you that after reading this book, you will not walk away from this passage with a feeling of defeat because we fall short of this perceived representation but will walk away with encouragement and pride. I'm eager for you to discover God's song of your heroism.

I'll join you with the first letter, *alef,* from Proverbs 31:10.

Pause and Reflect—Discussion Questions

1. Before this study, what were your initial thoughts on the verses of Proverbs 31:10–31?

   _____

   _____

   _____

   _____

2. What would you like to learn about the Proverbs 31 Woman passage?

   _____

   _____

   _____

   _____

3. What you know of the Proverbs 31 Woman might not apply to your present life, and you might feel as though you are already starting with a loss counted against you. Romans 8:1 tell us, "There is now no condemnation for those who are in Christ Jesus." Strong woman, are you willing to have an open mind and consider the next layer, a deeper understanding? How can God's voice of truth encourage you through Proverbs 31?

   _____

   _____

   _____

   _____

She Is as Strong as an Ox

Alef—the Ox

Proverbs 31:10

In Hebrew, Proverbs 31:10 begins with the word *ishah*, אִשָּׁה, which is "woman." Written Hebrew is read from right to left, so the first word of the verse begins with the letter א, or *alef*. As an acrostic poem, this letter and the word picture associated with it would trigger something in the reader's memory to help them recall the wisdom of the verse and how it applies to the woman.

Alef is associated with the representation of an ox. If you turn the English letter *A* upside down, you might recognize how the letter was written originally to resemble the head of an ox; over time the letter was flipped to the image we use today. Its extended meaning relates to leadership, strength, and sacrifice, and it holds the numeric value one, the number of total unity.[1]

Oxen are large animals trained for service to carry great weight. Even today we use the phrase "strong as an ox." Often two oxen were joined by a yoke to provide greater strength and endurance as a team. Even when yoked together, however, one of the oxen will naturally be the

---

1. See introduction to learn more about what it means for a Hebrew letter to hold numeric value.

dominant leader. With this image in mind, let's break down this verse phrase by phrase.

An Excellent Wife

To promote clarity and smooth translation from Hebrew to English, translators rearranged and added words to fit English grammatical rules:

> King James Version: Who can find a virtuous woman? For her price is far above rubies.
>
> New American Standard Bible: An excellent wife, who can find? For her worth is far above jewels.
>
> English Standard Version: An excellent wife who can find? She is far more precious than jewels.
>
> New International Version: A wife of noble character who can find? She is worth far more than rubies.
>
> The Message: A good woman is hard to find, and worth far more than diamonds.

Did you notice how this verse reads differently in each Bible version? Each translation is accurate, but the word choices were dependent on the culture and language of the times in which they were updated based on what would have made the most sense to the reader. The goal of the translator also influenced the word choice. Did they want a word-for-word translation or a thought-for-thought translation? In the Hebrew version of the verse, we see the woman described as *chayil*, which has most often been translated into English as "excellent," "virtuous," "noble," and "good."

As twenty-first century English speakers, most of us have learned a very different understanding of this word when compared to the actual Hebrew word. We tend to think of *virtuous* as being morally upright or chaste and *excellent* as good or worthy. However, more accurate translation of *chayil* means strength, valor, and force, not only of body but mind.

The word *chayil* appears 243 times in the Old Testament, and it is nearly always used as a reference to the military strength of men in warfare. It is most often translated as "an army," "power," "force," and "strength."[2] Throughout history, describing a woman as having the strength of a warrior would have been radical, yet we see here the memory trigger for a young man reciting these verses would essentially be: "When seeking a wife, find a woman of strength, as strong as an ox. Yoke yourself to her and become a working team."

While Torah scribes were familiar with the word *chayil* in relation to men, there are only two occasions in Scripture where this word is used to describe a woman, once here in Proverbs 31:10 and also in Ruth 3:11, where Ruth is described as a "woman of excellence." That word is *chayil*.

The *chayil* of the Proverbs woman, then, is best manifested in her focus on God. The woman described is not an overbearing woman with a strong personality who wields her control over others for her advantage; this behavior does not illustrate a woman of strength and value.[3] Instead, this woman understands she must live yoked to God.

A powerful understanding of *chayil* would be to consider it a word of blessing, celebration, and encouragement. Jewish families use Proverbs 31:10–31 as a song of blessing over the women of the house every Friday evening during Shabbat dinner. Shabbat is the Jewish holy day of rest. It begins with a celebration meal and blessing at sunset on Friday night and continues until sunset on Saturday.

Whatever your role in life, you can be confident of the strength bestowed on you through Christ. Whether a stay-at-home mom or

---

2. Lynette Woods, "Being Strong and Free," *Unveiling.org* (blog), February 14, 2013, https://unveiling.org/2013/02/14/being-strong-and-free/.

3. Ibid.

CEO, single or married, do all you do as a woman of valor and strength. When we accomplish goals or overcome a trying situation that requires the use of our mental or physical strength, a blessing of encouragement would be a proclamation of the phrase, *eshet chayil*, the opening phrase of Proverbs 31:10, "Woman of strength!" How would you feel having that proclaimed over you?

Who Can Find?

God inspired the author to begin the Proverbs 31:10–31 passage by reminding the young man that when seeking a wife, *alef* represents the first place, and God is always first. The first quality to look for in a wife is spiritual strength. He would want to find a wife who will honor God first. In finding this character in her, he would be looking to be equally yoked.

The author then asks, "Who can find?" This question suggests he isn't seeking an ordinary woman but one who is hard to find and finding her requires effort. Interestingly, Jewish scholars believe "the wife is an integral part of the husband. Therefore, until a man finds his mate, the woman is regarded as a 'lost' item."[4] One Jewish commentary offered that Psalm 32:6 is encouragement for men to pray before seeking "something lost," so that, with God's help, this item (or wife) of worth will be discovered. Isn't this a lesson we can all learn? Finding the right woman—or the right man—requires prayer. The one searching is like one seeking a lost part of himself.[5]

I met my husband almost as a dare to God. My previous relationship was destructive and chipped away at my self-worth. I remember crying out to God and swearing off all future men unless He brought along someone who met my long list of criteria. Little did

---

4. Matityahu Glazerson, *Building Blocks of the Soul: Studies on the Letters and Words of the Hebrew Language* (Northvale, NJ: Jason Aronson Inc., 1997), 178.
5. Ibid.

I know my husband would not only meet those requirements, but as a bonus God also blessed him with characteristics I never knew to ask for. The only problem was, he wasn't my "type" at all. I was seeking a fantasy, not the man God knew I would need. As my prayer life matured, so did my understanding of what makes a godly man. Thank God for that!

Do you realize Christ seeks a relationship with you in the same way? Jesus came to seek and save the lost (Luke 19:10), and He seeks us with the desire for us to become His worshippers (John 4:23).

For Her Worth Is Far above Jewels

When I was a little girl, I loved to visit my grandma's house and play dress-up in her silky flowing chiffon nightgowns. The sparkling "diamond" necklaces and earrings I adorned myself with may have been costume jewelry, but in my imagination, I was a regal princess. I just knew my prince would arrive one day and ask for my hand in marriage.

I wonder if the Proverbs woman had the same dream. So many little girls do. But my childhood was marred with abuse, neglect, and molestation. Those diamonds I wore at Grandma's soon mingled with dangling baubles of shame and worthlessness.

But Proverbs 31:10 tells men and their fathers to consider the value of this great woman of worth when figuring the transaction of marriage with her because she is a woman unlike any other. In keeping with the Ancient Near East custom of arranged marriages, paying a bride price was part of the arranged agreement.[6] Historically, however, the worth of a woman was not usually recognized or described like that of this Proverb 31 Woman. One commentary on

---

6. Ralph Gower, *The New Manners and Customs of Bible Times* (Chicago: Moody Press, 1996), 64.

this passage notes, "It is very remarkable to meet with such a delineation of a woman in the East, where the female generally occupies a most degraded position and is cut off from all sphere of activity and administration."[7]

Reading about this for the first time, I recalled those baubles of shame, and I wondered what my worth was—in both God's eyes and my husband's. God graciously reminded me that as the daughter of the King and a member of the family of Christ, I am held in uncommonly high esteem and worth, for I have been bought with a price (1 Corinthians 6:20). And so were you.

Indeed, a woman of strength is priceless, worth more than precious jewels. The Hebrew word translated as "jewels" in Proverbs 31:10 (or "rubies" in other translations) is *paniyn*. Many commentaries agree the word means a small round object that has a red tint, usually defined as coral or a pearl. The first time I read that definition of the word *paniyn*, I was immediately struck by how the description of small, round, red, and priceless objects resembled drops of blood, the precious red blood our Savior shed. As a woman of strength, you hold great value. You are so valuable to God He was willing to shed His precious blood for you. He paid this price for you; your worth is now far above rubies, pearls, or other jewels.

Oh, strong woman, God's Word describes you as fearfully and wonderfully made (Psalm 139:14). You are made in His image (Genesis 1:27). Pause and let that concept of love wash over you. Reflect on your worth in His eyes, on the price He was willing to pay, and enjoy for a moment the incredible value He sees in you.

----

7. Joseph S. Exell and Henry D. M. Spence-Jones, "Proverbs 31 Portrait of a Matron" in *Pulpit Commentary*. N.p.:n.d. Biblehub. https://biblehub.com/commentaries/pulpit/proverbs/31.htm Web. 18 Oct. 2015.

Alef's Song of Strength

To appreciate this acrostic poem, let's link our knowledge of *alef* and the meaning within the verse to our lives today. The passage describes a married woman, so there is first a link to marriage intended in this message. The Bible describes marriage as man and woman becoming one flesh, no longer two (Mark 10:8 and Ephesians 5:31). In Ecclesiastes 4:9–10, the writer encourages that "two are better than one because they have a good return for their labor. For if either of them falls, the one will lift up his companion."

The yoking related to *alef* is an example we can still use in marriage today. Just as oxen are yoked together to form a working team, husbands and wives are to be yoked together and united as one. There is strain on the marriage yoke when wives and husbands find themselves pulling in different directions instead of working as a team. When my prince arrived, I felt more like Cinderella sitting in the ashes of life rather than a princess on the throne of promise. My husband paid a great price for my hand in marriage. By then I had become quite the control freak with impossibly high standards for both myself and everyone around me, and I took my failures out on him. Our yoke of marriage was pulled in a zigzag pattern for several years.

If we had followed the example of *alef*, however, we would have understood the importance of the husband and wife yoking themselves first to Christ. Our marriage gained unity through Him. His strength must be part of the team. Jesus recognized the importance of being yoked to the Father for continued strength and unity. He tells us in John 10:30, "I and the Father are one." To be yoked indicates a position of total obedience and dedication.

As women, it is not uncommon to feel like the ox of our family or in daily living. We work to find a balance in caring and providing for others while still finding time to meet our needs. We will often work and serve to the point of sacrifice, including sacrificing our hopes, dreams, and careers. In doing so, we may find ourselves feeling unappreciated and tired. We question our worth and abilities. If we are married, we may even question the man to whom we are yoked.

If we depend only on our strength, we will eventually wear out. It is important to remember, as a believer in Christ, you are part of a working team with Christ, and team members draw on the strength of each other. Here in Proverbs 31:10, God describes us as strong. We are suited for the yokes we bear in life. But when we struggle under our burdens, we must recognize our need to depend on Jesus. Our burdens may be heavy, but we do not have to grow weary. Our yoke with Christ provides rest. He makes the burden light (Matthew 11:28–30). We can only do this as one who is serving by the strength God supplies (1 Peter 4:11).

Jesus patiently redirected me away from the zigzags in my life. He lifted my burdens and became my strength. My husband and I are now a well-defined, strong-working team. If our marriage was not firmly yoked to Christ, it would have failed. Only through our unity with Christ and our dependence on His leading as the strength of our team have we lasted twenty-eight years and counting.

My life has not been a fairy tale either, and because of my past I rarely felt I held the value of jewels. I often breathe in the words of Isaiah 62:4 as though they were written for me: "It will no longer be said of you, 'Forsaken,' nor to your land will it any longer be said, 'Desolate'; but you will be called 'My delight is in her.'" Add to this God's proclamation of my value here in Proverbs 31:10, and I feel the healing balm of His song deep into the depths of my being. Through Christ, I am *eshet chayil,* a woman of strength! You too are as strong as an ox and yoked to God. He will provide the strength and desire to serve according to His plan. Wherever you are in life, you have great value!

Consider this new understanding of *alef* as we explore Proverbs 31. When we read verse 10 with this new insight, we might understand it to say: God, like *alef,* is first, so yoke yourself to Him. You are rare and valuable, worth more than precious jewels and worthy of pursuit. Christ was willing to pay the price for you, and He shed His blood for you. Just as oxen are yoked in service, yoke yourself to Christ as you serve and sacrifice. Be united as one, and He will take the lead and provide you with His strength.

Take courage, strong woman, and know God acknowledges your value in Proverbs 31:10 as He proclaims over you, *eshet chayil,* "woman of strength!" Let that sink into your heart. Meditate on these words. The full blessing of Christ's strength is what is offered. Consider how you might fulfill the characteristics of *alef* through strength, service, sacrifice, and leadership.

Pause and Reflect—Discussion Questions

1. Before beginning this study, what were your initial thoughts on the verses of Proverbs 31:10–31?

_____

_____

_____

_____

2. To whom or what are you primarily yoked to for strength and leadership?

_____

_____

_____

_____

3. How would you define your life of service?

_____

_____

_____

_____

_____

4. In what ways do you sacrifice for others? Does it leave you feeling used, devalued, and resentful or satisfied and worthy?

_____

_____

_____

_____

5. What strength do you add to your family that God will proclaim *eshet chayil* over you? (This can be physical strength, spiritual strength, or strength of character, etc.)

_____

_____

_____

_____

_____

6. What women in your life would you describe as a woman of strength? Why?

_____

_____

_____

_____

_____

Praying the *Alef-Bet*

Lord, You are *alef.* You are the beginning, and there is none before You. Jesus, I pray I will yoke myself to You and be completely united with You. I pray Your Holy Spirit will strengthen me as I serve my family and those within my influence. Father, I pray I will joyfully sacrifice myself for Your service. Amen.

ב

She Invites Christ to Make His Home in Her Heart

Bet—the House

PROVERBS 31:11

My husband and I had the pleasure of building our first home. I'll admit we disagreed when it came to style choices and prioritizing the importance of upgrades. Overall, we enjoyed the experience, but who knew deciding where to put an electrical outlet could provoke an argument? I trust my husband to maintain the safety and maintenance of our homes. He wisely leaves the decorating to me. He also trusts me to establish traditions and set the rhythm in our home, an assignment so many of us have as wives, moms, and grand-mothers.

Bet represents the numeric value of two and the word picture of a house. You might recognize it in the Hebrew word *Bethlehem*, which means the "house of bread," or Bethel, which means "house of God." In biblical times, homes "were looked upon as a gift of God, and when a house was first built there was an act of dedication. . . . A home was not a place of possession . . . rather it is a place of welcome."[1] An old

---

1. Gower, *The New Manners and Customs of Bible Times*, 31, 41.

Jewish proverb takes this a bit further by declaring hospitality as a form of worship. As a house, *bet* relates to the Temple, the House of the Lord. God's dwelling place was an intricate part of Israel's life. The Israelites visited the Temple daily, considering it "the focal point of God's holiness on the Earth."[2] It was the only place they could adequately worship and reconcile themselves to God. The Spirit of God has since moved from the Temple and now makes His home in the hearts of believers, which lends to the imagery of *bet* also representing the heart.

In the Garden of Eden, God knew man should not live alone, so woman was created and the first household was established. In Jewish thinking, other than the Torah, the home is the most critical aspect of life. The Talmud teaches, "When a man gets married, this is the first time he merits the term 'man.'"[3] It was after God created both man and woman, and joined them together, that humankind received God's blessing (Genesis 1:28).

The flow of this Proverbs poem declares *alef*, a reminder that we are strong, valuable, and worthy of pursuit. Our responsibility is to first yoke ourselves to Christ. Nothing comes before Him. *Bet* adds the next step: the value of inviting Christ to make His home in our hearts as we make Him the heart of our home.

When you first encounter Samantha, she appears to have her life together. She has a fabulous thirty-year marriage, and her life seems smooth. At least that is what she would like you to believe. Those thirty years are packed with hard life lessons and the redeeming grace of God.

During an especially difficult time in her marriage, walls of independence grew into bulwarks of separations. Samantha began feeling

---

2. Dick Mills and David Michael, *Messiah and His Hebrew Alphabet: Studies in the Hebrew Alphabet with Messianic Overtones from Aleph—the Sacrifice—to Tav—the Cross* (Orange, CA: Dick Mills Ministries, 1994), 5.

3. Glazerson, *Building Blocks of the Soul*, 89.

the isolation that work, the demands of parenting, and the stresses of life often cultivate. Eventually the growing impasse between her and her husband became impossible to breach. She believed her life would only contain the mundane, and she had been forced to settle for much less than her dreams. Her love for her husband began a slow fade.

Another lie, cloaked in the attention of an old high school boyfriend, wormed its way through the tiniest crack of her resolve with devastating results. If you are married, how quickly do you recognize the warning signs when your affection and attention has waned? How do you respond? Samantha will admit, "I never thought I would be someone to sink into an affair. My actions shocked even me." Maybe your relationship with Christ is experiencing a similar shift. God warns against this in Revelation 2:4 when he tells the church at Ephesus they have left their first love. It happens subtly. Our Sundays become booked with activity. Friends move, and we lose fellowship. The church betrays us, so we don't attend as often. Suddenly we find ourselves settling. How would you rank your first-love commitment to Christ?

The Heart of Her Husband Trusts in Her

In following the acrostic format, the next word, בָּטַח, *batach,* the Hebrew word *trust,* begins with *bet.* This trust is strong. It means to adhere or to weld. I'm sure most couples would agree that when married, their goal is to build an unbreakable trust. One with the strength of a true weld.

The Bible uses this same word in Proverbs 3:5, which tells us to trust, *batach,* the Lord with all our hearts, more than our understanding. Trust in the home is essential, and the trust between a husband and wife has a direct effect on the strength of their marriage. This trust is similar to the trust between God and His followers.

Samantha's brief affair sent her headlong into a dark abyss. "My constant thought was that my husband would never forgive me. The lie kept telling me, 'You've gone this far, what does it matter if you go further and just leave him first?'"

She swallowed the lie that divorce was her only option. As the process began to churn through the life they had built, her husband asked her a question that struck like lightning, "Is this really what you want?" "No, it wasn't. This affair was the worst mistake of my life, but how could he ever forgive me?" In a vulnerable moment, her husband confessed he didn't know if their marriage would survive but suggested counseling as a start. If at the end she still wanted a divorce, they would move forward with dissolving their marriage.

The trust between Samantha and her husband lay exposed like rubble on a battlefield. Rebuilding a trust like *batach* comes with the risk of the unknown. In Proverbs 31:10 and 11, *alef* and *bet* represent the biblical establishment of a home through the union of marriage. God is first yoked to the believing husband and wife whose hearts trust in God. *This* type of home creates a sense of contentment, so much so that the hearts of the home have full confidence in each other. This is the home Samantha again worked toward.

The union of trust with God applies to everyone, married or single. Today, there are vast differences in homes and families. Our homes can be a place to define ourselves as we share, teach, and extend hospitality. One goal of a home is to reveal the peace and honor of a holy place such as the Temple. This is only possible as we yoke ourselves to God and trust in His leadership. What are some of the goals in your home? How do you develop trust with others and between you and God?

At their first counseling session, Samantha admitted the love she once felt for her husband had waned. The toll of their independent lives was steep. Eventually, over many tears and honest conversations, healing began, and the walls of isolation began to fall. Trust was still a seedling, but Samantha's husband loved her, and he was willing to try.

I know the sting of betrayal and how abandoned it can make us feel. God never shuts the door on a relationship with Him. He leaves a crack so we can push through and reencounter His heart of love for us. It is hard to trust and love again. I'm stubborn, and I want others to make the first move toward reconciliation. But God is welded into my heart, and where He goes, I'll follow. Even stumbling down the path of forgiveness. He forgives me, so I can forgive others. Where there is true repentance and sorrow, there can be forgiveness, and homes can be rebuilt. Has your trust been betrayed? Is your heart welded shut or is there a crack through which God can work?

Have you heard the saying "the heart of the home"? The Hebrew word for heart, *lebab*, has an interesting wordplay with the imagery, which I think applies to Proverbs 31:11. Heart is spelled *lamed* (word picture means leader) and *bet* (word pictures mean heart or home). These word pictures reveal the heart leads the home and what is inside. The imagery also illustrates two hearts, represented by *bet*, walking together. These can represent the hearts of the husband and wife but, even more, the heart of the believer walking with God. If we offer God a heart that requests Him, an attitude of love and trust will overflow into our home. Strong woman, 2 Chronicles 14:11 reminds us God is available to help those who have no strength. Psalm 9:10 promises those who put their trust in the Lord and seek Him will not be forsaken. When we are afraid, Psalm 56:3 encourages us to put our trust in God. Having a heart for God is reflected when God does not just visit the home but rather dwells in it.

Bet also represents the number two, the first number that can be divided into individuals that will stand alone. This creates the first opportunity for Satan and the world to work diligently to split and separate the power of the home.[4] We strive to build trust in our family,

---

4. E. W. Bullinger, *Number in Scripture* (Ravenio Books, 2015), PDF e-book, part II, "Two."

but it is even more important to trust in the Lord and to offer Him a heart He can trust in return. Only then can we begin to build godly homes. Satan works hard to divide the home. Ask yourself what you have done to make Christ the heart of your home.

And He Will Have No Lack of Gain

I mentioned that Proverbs 31 has a military theme. *Gain* in this verse is an example of that theme. It refers to spoils of war and, in this case specifically, the "spoil" of a wife as a reward. The husband's heart makes its home with his wife's heart. She is valuable to him, as is the trust he has in her. He no longer needs to plunder and seek other gains. He is content, and his heart can be at rest.

Trust grew between Samantha and her husband, but she will confess, "I occasionally have panic attacks if my plans get rerouted, I end up somewhere I didn't plan, and my husband doesn't know. I feel like he needs to know my every move. He doesn't ask for this, but a tiny foothold of lingering doubt can send me reeling. I pray that I never forget the pain I caused. I don't wallow in unforgiveness and my husband doesn't hold my actions as a threat over my head, but I never want to minimize my actions. The heart of my husband fully and completely trusts in me, and I never want to lose it again."

God wants a heart He can make His home in, one He trusts. He wants us to desire His plan for our lives. Sometimes our hearts are not in it, and we may feel defeated. We may face circumstances that test our strength physically, mentally, and spiritually. We will question our relationships and our abilities, and the very foundations of our home can shake. Your heart and your home may not reflect peace or trust, but it can. Your home may be chaotic, and your heart might be weary. God does not require perfection, only a heart He can trust, and those hearts come in a variety of offerings.

There are no perfect hearts, just like there are no perfect homes. God desires to use us, even in our imperfections. I genuinely believe that when God searches humankind to find someone He can trust to fulfill his plan, He looks at the hearts of believers, which reflect our imperfect lives and experiences. When we look at ourselves, we see flaws, blemishes, bruises, and scars from poor decisions or a difficult life. When God looks at us, He strips away what we consider flaws. He doesn't see them. God doesn't look to the outside. He looks to the heart (1 Samuel 16:7). God looks through our experiences.

As He makes His home in our hearts, He uses our experiences to develop compassion, forgiveness, love, and ultimately trust in us so we can share with others. The scars of our lives have been written on our hearts so that each of our unique, individual hearts is welded with His and is matched to His perfect plan. In the eyes of God, you have value, He trusts you, and you can rest in Him. In His grace God uses us with all our imperfections to establish a godly, trusting heart. Pause a moment. What do you consider to be the biggest struggle you face that prevents you from fully trusting God or keeping your focus consistently on Him? You can't begin to deal or heal if you don't identify it. Trust, *batach*, God. Through a relationship with him, our hearts are changed.

Pause and Reflect—Discussion Questions

1. How would you describe the tone of your home?

_____

_____

_____

_____

2. What have you done to make Jesus the heart of your home?

_____

_____

_____

_____

_____

_____

3. Because of your life circumstances is it hard to put your trust in others? If so, how has this affected your trust in God?

_____

_____

_____

_____

_____

_____

4. What is one change you can make in your home to help it reflect God?

_____

_____

_____

_____

_____

5. How does knowing you are a strong woman affect your perception of whether you have the strength and ability to make the changes in your heart needed to create trust in your home?

_____

_____

_____

_____

_____

Praying the *Alef-Bet*

Jesus, bless my home. I pray that my heart puts You first and my home is a peaceful, holy sanctuary for all who enter. Father, give me a heart for forgiveness as I honor others. Help me to create a home that has the environment of trust and safety that reflects Your heart. In the name of Jesus, amen.

א

She Carries the Benefit
of Kindness

Gimel—the Camel

Proverbs 31:12

When I traveled to Israel, one goal was to ride a camel. During a stop outside of Jericho, I had my chance as a local led tourists on his camel slowly around a parking lot. I hesitated. I wanted something more authentic. Camels were not meant to be led in circles like a circus sideshow, but I didn't know if I would get another opportunity. I took a risk and declined. Later, when we arrived at the mysterious desert city of Petra, my gamble paid off. As the camel knelt into the red sand, I climbed aboard. We easily maneuvered through the ruins of Petra, which were carved into the rose-colored mountains. I realized how valuable this quirky, misunderstood animal was for the trade caravans of long ago.

Camels are known to assist weary travelers while carrying the weight of valuable products through vast distances in harsh conditions. Camels must kneel to be loaded with goods at the onset of their journey, then again to unload when they reach their destination. The service a camel provides as a burden bearer influenced the development of *gimel's* word picture, which is a camel. *Gimel* is also known as a bridge, likely because of the camel's hump, and is considered a conduit of kindness.

Some imagine the shape of the letter resembles a camel's foot. The Talmud offers this foot is a reminder to run after those less fortunate in spirit and extend our knowledge of God so they can experience His loving-kindness, or *chesed*, a word that is much deeper than simply being pleasant. It holds the ideas of unchanging love, mercy, and grace. As a conduit or bridge of God's *chesed*, we can help others until they are ripe spiritually and can stand on their own, another teaching of *gimel*.

Read Proverbs 31:12 again and add this new layer of *gimel*. Think of how these qualities are woven into marriage and create a godly home. At first glance, it appears the Proverbs 31 Woman is busy doing good, and her family benefits from her actions. A word study suggests a little more. Proverbs 31:12 starts with the letter *gimel*, which represents the uplifting kindness of a camel, in the word *gamal*, which means a benefit, to treat a person well, to ripen, to deal bountifully. The idea of reward developed from *gamal*.

Like the camel, the Proverbs woman is an added benefit to her family; even more, she is their reward. What benefits do you offer? Who can benefit from your uplifting kindness?

She Will Do Him Good and Not Evil

As a full-time pastor, it is easy to see the principles of the Proverbs 31 Woman at work in Juana's life. But Juana is a single woman who has never married. Doesn't this passage only apply to married women? Juana shares, "I'd love to have a partner in ministry and the support of a husband, but it has not happened yet. And my commitment to Christ comes before anything else. I have a lot of love, and I share it with those Jesus puts in my path." Married or single, this is the commitment needed to personify the qualities of *gimel*. The good we offer others reflects our experience of His loving-kindness.

In Hebrew, the second word in Proverbs 31:11 is *towb,* translated as "good." *Towb* is a beautiful word. Several pieces of Jewish literature suggest the word carries a musical connotation with the idea of being in tune or harmony. Imagine the sweet melody of walking in harmony with Jesus. The Holy Spirit is our *gimel* and bridge to God. He fine-tunes our relationship.

As I work with Juana in ministry, I am struck by her boldness, but her softer side bears the burdens for the many she serves. For some, she is the first bridge they encountered when experiencing God's acceptance and loving-kindness. Often my time with Juana begins with her recounting a recent encounter she had with complete strangers—the woman who needed help moving, so Juana organized assistance, the young man considering ministry work, so Juana directed him to a youth mission project and a potential mentor, or the young pregnant mother Juana encountered while leading a prayer walk through a blighted downtown area, so she arranged a community baby shower for her. On another prayer walk Juana met a homeless man who poured out his pain and allowed her to pray for him. These are all opportunities to bridge the gap between the people she encounters and the God who loves them.

How do *you* act as a bridge of God's loving-kindness? The Bible provides us with these reminders of His kindness:

> Galatians 5:22 lists kindness as a component of the fruit of the
> Spirit of God within us.
> 1 Corinthians 13:4 notes that love is kind.
> Job 6:14 instructs that a despairing man should be shown kindness,
> so that he does not forsake the fear of the Almighty.
> Psalm 143:8 proclaims that as we respond to God's kindness with
> trust, He lifts our soul.

Like the camel, the Proverbs woman benefits others by using intentional acts of kindness to lift and carry them until they can stand on their own.

Others can make it difficult to extend God's loving-kindness. Juana would know. As a Black woman she experiences the ugliness of fractured racial relationships. An elementary classroom was the setting in which she first experienced the bitter sting of a racial slur her classmate flung at her in contempt. Juana is educated and speaks with authority, but she is also funny, giving, and loving. Juana shared, "My mother affirmed my worth and value daily, but that one word had a profound impact on me, even then. I am a proud, strong black woman, but God's love for me was overshadowed by a label."

Labels start young. I work with hundreds of teenagers who fling them like confetti. They are collected, and the enemy eagerly nurtures them. What labels have grown to define you? Lifting another can simply be a spoken word of affirmation, which strips away the enemy's lies and bridges the gap between someone's despair and God's love. Something we can all benefit from.

The depth of God's love bloomed for Juana when she encountered other young black college students who loved God fiercely. They did not allow society's curse from the color of their skin to erase His truth. Juana recognized she was not like them. "I wanted their depth of faith. God beckoned me and drew me in. Not everyone experiences the loving affirmation I received. I encounter so many who need kindness."

Juana works to bridge the gaps many face in their lives—socially, racially, and spiritually. She willingly accepts the mission of reconciling black and white. But her greater calling is to reconcile the entire diverse body of Christ so they in turn will be a bridge of reconciliation for others. May I encourage you to pause here and spend some time in prayer? Ask God to reveal His strength for you as you encounter opportunities to extend His *chesed* and act, as Juana does, bridging the gaps of race, financial inequity, and social divides. How is He prompting you?

When kindness is the last virtue we wish to offer, we need to remember God "has not dealt with us according to our sins, nor rewarded us according to our iniquities" (Psalm 103:10). It is interesting to note the word *rewarded* used in Psalm 103:10 (or *treat, dealt,* or *repay* in other versions) is the word *gimal,* the same word used to begin Proverbs 31:12. When we repay someone, we often base our response on their past actions. Psalm 103:10 is a potent reminder that it is through God's loving-kindness that we do not receive the recompense we are owed if dealt with according to our sins.

A strong woman makes the active choice to respond by doing good and not evil all the days of her life. I'm the first to admit this is hard. One time the principal at the school where I worked offered our faculty a bingo game to play during the month of November. As we completed suggested acts of kindness for others, we checked off squares. It was a game to be used to encourage team building. It was sweet . . . and it stressed me out. When I caught myself thinking this game was just another list I had to complete, I felt like such a loser! The flow of the Proverbs 31 poem reminded me God's loving-kindness is only accomplished through my relationship with Christ. It isn't a to-do list but a choice in my heart to honor God. Yes, we blow it. Yes, we will fail at times, but I'm encouraged to know God doesn't repay me according to my failures. He provides His blueprint of strength, and His *chesed,* so it can be said of us all, "She does him good and not evil all the days of her life."

All the Days of Her Life

This portion of the verse leads to *gimel's* meaning to nourish until completely ripe and to wean, as mentioned earlier. If you are any type of caretaker, you understand this concept. It may be difficult to accept, but the role of a mother is to teach children independence so she will no longer be needed. She helps them until they are ripe and can stand on their own. I can relate, but I sometimes take it too far. I think I can do things better and quicker, and, frankly, it is often easier just to do a task instead of taking the time to teach someone or to accept the result. When I do this with my children, it's at the expense of their learning a necessary skill or life lesson. I struggle to remember when to say when.

What needs of others do you encounter daily? Do you tend to take on their burdens? How can you lift them up while helping them stand on their own? At some point, we need to stop taking on their burdens as our own and instead allow them to ripen physically and spiritually. As we do this, we can enjoy God's blessing of harmony.

Gimel's Song of Strength

Perhaps lifting others is hard because of our own burdens. We have enough to carry. We can't take on more. Some of us feel we don't have much to offer, and some may struggle with perfectionism. How do you define perfect? Do you think perfect equals flawless? One biblical definition for perfect is complete, entire, or full. This gives me a new perspective. I don't have to be flawless or perfect to be complete and useful to God.

The banana is an excellent example of this idea. A banana grows until it reaches a certain size. Even though it continues to ripen, its growth is complete. It is usable throughout all ripening stages. As a young, green banana, it can be cooked in recipes. It is tastiest as a yellow, middle-aged banana. And when it turns brown, it is preferred for baking. In all stages, it is a banana, perfect for its different uses. Women are like bananas. We have many benefits to offer in all stages of our lives. But we may tend to seek flawless perfection at the expense of complete usefulness.

Juana's assignment as senior pastor at her current church allows her to be used to span a gulf of racism. Her church is located blocks away from a historic slave market. Her city holds deep roots in the civil rights movement and fought against integration in the early 1960s. It was once described as the most racist city in America. Juana believes God placed a calling on her life. Her dream is to build a church that will be a multiethnic body of Christ bridging social classes and races.

She explains, "My focus is prayer, preaching, and pointing others to Christ." But even as she does that, an undercurrent of racism can still be felt. "One well-wisher I encountered patted my arm and said, 'We need more people like you.' I can choose how I react to that. I can take it as a reference to my skin color or the fact that I'm a female senior pastor. I'd like to think the area needs more people like me who are bold, who will speak for Jesus, who will pray fervently and connect them to Christ. I can't go to that dark place. The God I serve is too important."

When yoked to Christ, our actions and attitudes can be a channel of God's good and can help others bear up the weight of life's difficulties as they travel through times that seem like a dry, weary land. Their burdens can deplete us as well. Christ is our source of living water, through whom we can replenish all that we pour into others. Like a camel, we too kneel before God to have our burdens lifted. Only then can we be reloaded with blessings to carry to others.

If we desire to be an example of *gimel* we need to put aside the burdens of the world and our ideas of flawless perfection. Instead, store up refreshment and encouragement through God's Word and encountering His great love for us. His strength will help us endure the dry spells. Pause for a moment and consider how God's Word refreshes you. Thank Him for being our great reward and pray the joy of your salvation is restored and will sustain you (Psalm 51:12). You may even want to list the benefits you have personally experienced from your relationship with Jesus Christ.

Pause and Reflect—Discussion Questions

1. For whom do you have a spiritual burden? What burdens are you
   carrying that require the uplifting support of God?

   _____

   _____

   _____

   _____

   _____

2. At what times in your life have you seen the value of being on your
   knees before God?

   _____

   _____

   _____

   _____

   _____

3. What does God's loving-kindness look like in your life?

   _____

   _____

   _____

   _____

   _____

4. Do you have perceived imperfections in your life that you feel keep you from serving others? How does knowing the different stages of ripening help?

_____

_____

_____

_____

_____

5. What benefit do you offer your family?

_____

_____

_____

_____

Praying the *Alef-Bet*

Lord, thank You for bearing the burden of my sin and extending Your loving-kindness to me. Father, Your strength and Your Word are a refreshing benefit when I face dry and weary times in my life. Remind me of all the benefits I have gained through Your Son and help me to be a bridge for others to receive those same benefits.

ד

She Lives a Life Set Apart

Dalet—the Door

PROVERBS 31:13

Rebekah was an all-American girl next door, complete with blonde hair and enviable athletic skill developed from copious hours on the soccer field. Her talent was rewarded with college scholarship opportunities, but they came with the arduous lesson that seeking to honor God in life often requires sacrifice.

The written image of *dalet*, which begins verse 13, resembles an animal hide hanging from the lintel, a home's entrance. *Dalet's* word picture is a door, and through this open door, our path in life is revealed, and the world is wide open for us. *Dalet's* numeric value is four, which references creation. Think of it this way. There are four seasons: winter, spring, summer, and fall. The moon has four primary phases: new, waxing, full, and waning. The number four is commonly linked to creation. Can you think of other fours in nature?

She Looks for Wool and Flax

At one time in history, making yarn was necessary for adding the comforts in life. It has since transitioned into a hobby. I don't know how to knit, and my fumbling fingers have only mastered two basic crochet stitches. My daughter creates beautiful blankets. One Christmas she crocheted all the little girls in our family mermaid tails. Sadly, she did not learn this skill from me. YouTube was her teacher. Yet the Word of God must still apply to women today. Knowing *dalet* references creation helps us recognize that Proverbs 31:13 signals a new teaching topic for the strong woman. This fourth verse tells us she now must leave the door of her home and face God's created world. Isn't it interesting that in God's providence, the first three verses of the passage provide her with the trinity of strength before she faces the world? *Alef* represents God the Father, whom she is yoked to. Jesus then makes His home (*bet*) in her heart, and the Holy Spirit, *gimel*, is God's conduit of loving-kindness and lifts her as the link between God's spiritual world and His creation.

Years of honing her soccer skills earned Rebekah the pursuit of several college teams. She grew up in a loving, Christian home, which provided her a firm foundation like the Proverb woman's. Rebekah wanted to continue her education at a Christian college, and when a few schools offered her scholarships, she immediately began praying through her choices. One college flew her in for a tryout, but when she met the coach, she interpreted her discomfort as a warning. "The scholarship money was great, but for a Christian college, the coach was not very Christlike. By the end of the tryout, I decided the school wasn't for me. We are called to be set apart, and I wouldn't compromise my beliefs, even for a scholarship. I had to seek another opportunity."

This verse begins with the Hebrew word דרשׁ, *darash,* which means to search and seek with diligence and, in particular, with the goal to worship. I recognize a bit of wordplay in this verse. *Darash,* and the items the Proverbs woman is seeking, may suggest a reminder of how the nation of Israel was to live in the Promised Land. They were to pursue Jehovah in worship but remain set apart from other nations.

Wool and flax are a spiritual reference to the priestly garments used in Israel's worship. As part of ceremonial washing, the priests put on garments made of linen to symbolize their cleanliness (Leviticus 16:4). Wearing linen implied Israel's priests were different, and it separated them from the surrounding culture. Linen is made from fibrous flax stems that are rough on the hands and can even draw blood. Flax must be threshed out and then soaked in water to separate the fibers and make it easier to work into linen. Even then, linen only becomes soft after much use. Wool, being from an animal, represents the flesh. The lanolin in wool is soothing to the hands as it is spun. Knowing the materials wool and linen were never to be mixed as part of the priestly garments (Deuteronomy 22:11) underscores the idea of separation.

How do you live out God's command to follow His standards and not the world's? Sometimes life's red flags help us recognize a need to choose. Other times, we seek guidance from the Holy Spirit. This is what Rebekah did. "I had to acknowledge my gut feeling and stop to seek the Lord's prompting. When I did, I sensed Him telling me to be bold and speak up. I shook with fear as I questioned the coach's behavior. I shared my surprise at the language he used around the team. The coach brushed off my concerns. He encouraged the team to make me feel welcome, but I held firm. As I returned home in tears, I knew the scholarship offer was rescinded. I consoled myself knowing I was obedient, and I did not want to attend that college."

Rebekah is a strong woman of God. She found the balance between having a firmly set faith and a soft heart for following God, but only because she did the hard work of threshing out the harsh and the rough. Living a set-apart life is not accomplished because of walls built or lines drawn but rather out of love and devotion for Christ. Facing God's world as a door to life involves so much more.

After visiting several teams, Rebekah received additional offers. She faithfully prayed about her final decision and was surprised at God's direction. "The Lord kept telling me I had to go back to that first school or I'd miss a huge door of opportunity. The soccer team for that school was picked more for their ability than their Christian values. I wrestled with my decision. I listed every reason not to go, but when I finally understood that it was my chance to share Christ with them, I had to swallow my pride and call the coach. I asked if I could be a walk-on without a scholarship." Obedience is hard when you don't know the outcome, but if we are to live out the calling God puts before us, we take those tentative steps.

How do you consider your choices in life? Do you make a list of the pros and cons? Do you confer with others and seek advice? I do both, but Rebekah's story challenges me to realize that my list of pros and cons and good advice may not reveal God's plan. His way is not always our way. The question is, am I willing to accept His answer no matter how painful and hard the work might be?

Wool and flax symbolize a contrast between the soothing nature of our flesh and the world, as well as the righteous linen of God's kingdom. To prevent us from easing into the enticements of this world, we need to soak ourselves in the living waters of Jesus and thresh out our decisions, bad habits, and sin. Sometimes we don't want to do the hard work, which may include surrendering people, jobs, and the pleasures of life to get to a soft point in our life in Christ without it feeling rough or restrictive.

Rebekah's first year in college was the worst she had ever endured. The coach and the team treated her with contempt. "I did all the grunt work. It was my job to pick up after every game, gathering equipment and laundry. The college employed people to do this, but it seemed I was targeted, and it was required of me. I performed every task with hustle. No matter their treatment, I was respectful, and I did what was asked. I would never disappoint them or give them an opportunity to find fault. But after every practice or game, I returned to my dorm before I allowed the flood of my emotions to let loose. I was alone and miserable."

A strong woman understands that she straddles the doorway between kingdom and worldly living. God provides us with everything we need in His created world. God uses wool as an example of His boundaries and how we interact with the world's offerings. He wants us to use and enjoy what He provides, but His Word reminds us to love Him and not the things in the world (1 John 2:15–17). We must live in God's world but reflect His holiness. Honestly, there will be days this is painfully necessary.

Rebekah worked hard and was rewarded with a starting position in several games. She had every reason to believe the starting trend would continue when she learned her team would play a game in her home state. She took the opportunity to invite her family to come watch the game. "I shared my excitement with my teammates and coach. My family traveled to see us play, but I never played a minute. We lost. My coach benched me with no explanation, and yet again, I was left to clean up."

How does one live in the world and not become of the world? Living set apart doesn't mean you are alienated from others unlike you. When facing persecution like Rebekah did, sliding into the realm of isolation and judgment is tempting. In nature, the place where two rivers meet is called a confluence. The two rivers run parallel without mingling because of their differences in speed, density, and temperature. Google it. It is an incredible sight. The rivers are like oil and water. They don't blend. As we live in this world, we will meet others vastly different from us. The laws of nature and, even more, God require us to move alongside them, without taking on their qualities.

Christ knew living set apart from the world would be difficult for us. Our flesh is weak, and we have an enemy who diligently pursues us. Jesus prayed for us in John 17:15–17 when He asked His Heavenly Father to keep us from the evil one because we are not of this world.

Jesus warned in John 15:19 that if we accept the worldly trappings as our own, the world will love us, but in living a life of separation, the world will hate us.

Strong woman, His truth purifies us to recognize the deceptive, soothing nature of the world. *Dalet* is our reminder the Messiah is the door through which we leave the desires of this world and seek to enter His kingdom. With that, "We must pause in our busy lives to anticipate the many little *Daleths* or doorways that God will open to share with us the things of the spirit, fill what is lacking or deficient in the physical world, to take the poverty of this physical world and fill it with the blessings of God's spirit."[1] These *dalets* may be extreme like Rebekah faced. They may also be the Holy Spirit's prompting to check on a friend, to drop off supplies at a homeless shelter, to mow your elderly neighbor's yard, to make that phone call, to offer that smile. How easily do you recognize God's doors of opportunity while walking in this world?

And Works with Her Hands in Delight

The second half of verse 13 spotlights the attitude of those set apart in holiness. We are to act with *chephets,* a Hebrew word often translated as willing, to take pleasure, or, as in the NASB, delight. This Scripture tells us the strong woman delights in her work. She recognizes the value of her task.

Scripture confirms this attitude in several places.

> Our willing spirit is sustained through the joy of our salvation (Psalm 51:12)
> Willingly we sacrifice to God and give Him thanks (Psalm 54:6)

---

1. Chaim Bentorah, *Hebrew Word Study: Beyond the Lexicon* (Bloomington, IN: Tafford Publishing, 2014), 69.

> When we delight ourselves in the Lord, He gives us the desires of our hearts (Psalm 37:4)

Rebekah desired to delight in Christ, so she took another step of faith. "I felt encouraged to lead a Bible study, and I invited the team. No one came. I couldn't let that stop me. I did it again, and five girls came. One commented that I was a different kind of Christian, and it challenged her ideas of Christianity. She came because she had questions. She eventually became a believer, and we keep in touch today." Rebekah wanted nothing more than to blend in and be accepted at her college, but she remembered who she represented. How have you succeeded in removing the influences of the world? What areas are you still contending with, and where can you willingly choose God? Strong woman, remember wool and flax. You have God's trinity of strength backing you.

Dalet—Song of Strength

Dalet teaches us to thresh out the influences of the world so we can be holy. The Hebrew letters in the word holy, *qodesh,* contain the imagery of that which follows threshing at the door. Ladies, we are the doorkeeper of our homes. Doorkeepers are more than someone who merely welcomes others. The Bible identifies the doorkeeper's position as someone who stands at the entrance to the Temple to collect the tithes and offerings. They were also positioned at the entrance of the court of the high priest to protect the holiness of the Tabernacle (Numbers 25:11–13). Although men primarily filled this position, the Bible does recognize women who held this position (John 18:16–17; Acts 12:13). As a doorkeeper to your home and heart, how do you thresh at the entrance to protect the holiness of your sanctuary? Are there habits to be changed or items to be removed?

At one point in my walk with Christ, I realized my confession of sin had become lacking. Sure, I asked for forgiveness. "And dear Lord, please forgive my sins, amen." But I had no remorse. If pressed, I probably couldn't name a specific sin, its effect, or its consequences. Thankfully, this bothered me. Sin is ugly and destructive like that. I recognized that I should mourn over my sin, which nailed Christ to that Cross. My prayer life took an abrupt turn. I asked God to give me an acute awareness of my sin, all of it. I wanted to see it as He did. If I am to live a life of separation, the pull of sin shouldn't be compelling but rather repulsive. I haven't fully mastered my flesh. I'm struggling right along with you, and I continue to thresh it out of my life. With God's strength, I can now walk away from sin that once gave me pause. Can you identify sin in your life that you can now walk away from too?

Rebekah caught herself looking back and doubting her choices. She claims Philippians 3:13–14 as her life verse, and she interprets it this way, "I have to forget what lies behind and reach forward to what lies ahead and press on. I know if I look at my past, I'm tempted to dwell on what I should have done better. Instead, I look ahead at what God is calling me to do." When we focus on the disappointment or the struggle rather than God's calling, we miss God's plan. When seeking God's doors, we must know which reveal His calling. We must also accept that His doors are not always stately and new with shiny brass knockers. Sometimes they are worn and splintered, but He is always there to greet us. Remember the coach Rebekah played under? Later in life she applied for a coaching job and reached out to him for a referral. He wrote to Rebekah and apologized for how he treated her. He too became a believer in Jesus Christ and revealed to Rebekah that her character left a profound impact that never left him. *Eshet Chayil!*

In the next verse, Proverbs 31:14, we further explore how the strong woman faces the world. Please open the door of your heart and ask the Holy Spirit to walk with you. He has already prepared your way. I pray you do this with willing delight.

Pause and Reflect—Discussion Questions

1. As you walk in this world, will you be identified as set apart or do you blend in?

_____

_____

_____

_____

_____

2. Describe a time when you opened the door of your heart to someone quite unlike you.

_____

_____

_____

_____

_____

3. When dealing with something big we often pray, "Lord, open or close a certain door," but do you live in such a way that you will recognize the unlikely _dalets_? If not, how can this be changed?

_____

_____

_____

_____

_____

4. How can you willingly live a life of holiness knowing it may drive a
   wedge into a relationship with a friend, family member, or coworker?

_____

_____

_____

_____

_____

Praying the *Alef-Bet*

Lord Jesus, thank You for being the door through which I have access
to God. I pray that I will recognize Your path through this world that
You have prepared for me. I pray that as I travel this path, I will gladly
live a life that shows me to be set apart for You. Amen.

ה

She Is Moved by the Holy Spirit

Hei—the Window, Behold

PROVERBS 31:14

The oldest meaning of *hei* is "behold" or "here it is," but the letter's symbolism also extends to air, light, life, and the presence of God near us. In Hebrew, *hei* is revered. It is often a reference to the Spirit or the breath of God. The Bible tells us in Psalm 33:6 that the heavens came into being by the breath of God; this is *hei*. Knowing this helps us understand the memory trigger word for this verse, which is *hayah*. It means to come into being, to become, be in existence.

The shape of the letter has a small opening, or window, at the top left. Over time the word picture for *hei* developed into a window. This window reminds us of God's grace. As we behold our sin and its devastating effect, God always provides us with a window of return.

To pronounce *hei* you merely exhale breath with no sound from the throat. Linguists believe the Hebrews were likely the first people group to use the letter *hei* as a mark of their dedication to God.[1] In the Ancient Near East, *elym* was a common word for god, any god. Linguists sug-

---

1. Joel M. Hoffman, *In the Beginning: A Short History of the Hebrew Language* (New York, NY: New York University Press, 2004), 41.

gest the word *Elohim,* a Hebrew name of God, "clearly . . . refers to *the* Hebrew God . . . [it] is the word *elym* with the *heh* inserted to mark the word as belonging to the Hebrews" (emphasis added).[2] *Hei,* and its meaning, *behold,* noted that Elohim was beheld differently from the surrounding gods of their world.

The holy name God, Yahweh, is also spelled YHWH. This four-letter spelling is known as the Tetragrammaton. YHWH is spelled as it's pronounced, and like *hei,* with only breath. Isn't it humbling to know every breath we take to maintain our lives speaks the name YHWH? Try it, breathe in YA, breathe out WH. The Spirit of God made you, and the breath of the Almighty gives you life (Job 33:4).

As the strong woman walks through her door, she beholds the created world that reveals the possessive mark of *Elohim.* His breath fills her and marks her as His (Ephesians 1:13 NIV). Behold the breath of His Spirit as it hovers protectively over her.

She Is Like Merchant Ships

Growing up, Joy was immersed in a Christian atmosphere from kindergarten through college, and she even met her husband in her church's youth group. "He was great. We had the same circle of friends. He was a believer and served in the military. We were friends for three years before we started dating, and we were engaged for a year. I knew him well." Or so she thought. As her story spilled out, she revealed, "Before the honeymoon was over, I knew things were not as they seemed." Joy spent the next thirteen years in the clutches of emotional and mental abuse. "He was controlling, degrading, and demeaning, constantly accusing me. He was so covert. Outside the home, everyone thought he was fantastic. I hid my pain. I never shared what was happening to

---

2. Ibid. The Hebrew letters are spelled differently because of Greek and Yiddish influence, post-captivity translation, and the process of transliteration from Latin. Although spelled differently they are pronounced the same and hold the same word picture imagery.

me at home." Joy moved through deep waters of uncertainty, and for a time did not know from where to draw her resources.

During biblical times, merchant ships carried a variety of goods around the world. Israel was not a seafaring nation. As an agrarian and Sephardic culture, it was a steady consumer of traded products from the ports of Tyre, Sidon, Egypt, Phoenicia, and beyond. Trade ships from these distant ports moved as the prevailing winds pushed against sails and propelled them to their destinations. When identified as a part of God's household, His *bet,* the Holy Spirit becomes a channel, our *gimel,* of God's benefits. When Christ breathes His Holy Spirit, *hei,* into us, we receive His power, and we are propelled by the very breath of God to live our life for Christ. The presence of His Spirit is the necessary blessing we draw on to be the strong women He designed us to be.

As a stormed brewed within her marriage, Joy earnestly sought God to determine what direction to move in. "I began to learn the necessary boundaries I needed to navigate my husband's volatile demands since he would not accept treatment or medical help." But he figured out how to circumnavigate those boundaries.

God became Joy's anchor. She returned to Him, repeatedly crying out for healing and reconciliation. "God's steady and comforting voice kept telling me, 'Just stay with Me. Do not look to the left or the right.' It was like going across a tightrope blindfolded. I had to move with purpose. I couldn't hurry. Every step was slow and steady. I had to trust God, and He used that time to build my trust in Him." Joy and her husband sought counseling, but sharing her heart provided Joy's husband with more ammunition to use against her when they returned home. Within the first few sessions, her counselor recognized the danger she was in and encouraged separation.

How have you maintained boundaries in your difficult relationships? How have you depended on God's discernment and guidance? *Hei,* for us, is a reminder to behold God as we navigate our struggles and allow the Holy Spirit to gently propel us through those uncertain waters instead of being blown about by the winds of our circumstances.

Ships have small windows that allow light in and provide an opening to view the outside. In biblical times, a crisscross lattice often covered these windows and acted as a sieve by filtering out unwanted items. *Hei* is God's reminding whisper to sift and filter what we allow to flow through our minds and into our lives through the wisdom of the Holy Spirit. With counseling and the Holy Spirit's discernment, Joy realized something was very wrong with her husband. Joy refers to this time as her year of *surrender*, a word that peppered her journal entries. "One day in prayer I felt the Lord asking me, 'Will you surrender the outcome? Do you trust Me enough?' I froze. I knew I wanted this beautiful story of redemption, but I finally came to a place where I could surrender the outcome. I knew the only way out was to go through the darkness." Have you ever faced a similar time? How did you surrender the result to God?

The Bible notes two occasions when Satan stood before the throne of God and asked to directly impact believers—Job and Peter. Satan wanted to test their faith and commitment, and God allowed it. In Peter's case, Jesus stated Satan asked to "sift" Peter like wheat (Luke 22:31). To sift you need a sieve or filter, which will separate coarse material from the more delicate, softer material. Satan hoped to sift Peter to expose him as course material unworthy of use.

I have a feeling these are not the only two people Satan has requested to filter his attack. He actively seeks those he can destroy. It is vital we sift what Satan and the world offers so we can separate their course and unworthy offerings from the fine offerings of Christ. God's sifting in Joy's life provided her with a pastor and church staff that completely insulated her and agreed to walk the journey with her. Her purposeful steps with God were ordered with a grace she extended to her husband. Even as he was diagnosed with a personality disorder, hope remained. Joy shares, "The Lord pressed Job 31:6 on me. I wanted God to know my integrity." How do you cling to hope? Does reading your Bible help? Music? Prayer? Who can you call on to insulate you in prayer and encouragement? It is so tempting to allow anger and bitterness to rise to the top as we filter through our circumstances. Our only hope is to surrender ourselves to God's leading. It isn't easy. It can even be downright scary. But His anchor will hold as He brings about the winds of change in our lives.

She Brings Her Food from Afar

The word translated as "food" in verse 14 is *lechem*. Another translation is "bread." Think of the word *Bethlehem*. *Bet* (house) *lechem* (bread)—the house of bread. If the Proverbs woman lived in the rocky Judean hills, she would have procured grain for her household bread from the Jezreel Valley, considered Israel's breadbasket. Trade ships carried more exotic food choices. Proverbs 31:14 suggests the woman of strength is willing to go the distance to provide for her family and offer them a variety, but don't miss that she is providing her family with the most basic sustenance, the bread of life.

Joy clung to God's Word as her bread of life and took tentative steps until ultimately she was served with divorce papers. Alone, she slept with her Bible on the pillow next to her. "God pressed into my heart that He was my husband. My Bible reminded me that God alone would sustain me." Joy and her children began seeing a counselor through this process. "I also got rid of all distractions. I stripped our schedule down to the bare bones, and we spent time together. My husband eventually abandoned our children and me. I wanted my kids to know they were loved and secure. They had my full attention, to make good memories and experience laughter, as we dealt with the repercussions."

What are you feeding your family? I don't mean what type of cook are you, but what are you spiritually feeding your family? How are you sustaining them? The Bible offers us healthy menu suggestions because we cannot live by bread alone (Matthew 4:4). We strengthen our minds and bodies when we eat a healthy diet and not grow dependent on junk food. Have daily responsibilities worn you down to the point you settle for fast food? Do you sometimes feel like dried up, hard, and crusty bread as a woman, a mother, a wife? What can you do, even now, to renew your strength?

We cannot grow weary and lose heart (Galatians 6:9). Too much depends on our strength if we are to filter life's experiences and struggles. Taste and see that the Lord is good (Psalm 34:8). Jesus is our bread of life (John 6:35). By inviting the breath of the holy God to enter our dry bones and return us to life (Ezekiel 37:1–14), we can be propelled to continue.

During the divorce proceedings, Joy discovered buried secrets. Her husband had moved money from their joint account, and she was left with their family's financial burdens. Satan's constant accusations made her weary. "My thoughts were plagued with. 'You're divorced, what can you offer others? You're a failure.'" As she slowly relinquished her circumstances to God, it dawned on her how much energy drained from her as she tried to control or manipulate the outcome.

Do you succumb to Satan's lies in your struggle? Use God's Word, your Bread of Life, as your plumb line and filter. Even in your most difficult season, you have opportunity to behold God's goodness. As ships travel the sea, they often encounter strong storms, like our storms in life. Ours are accompanied with the surging surf of anxiety. We must anchor ourselves to Christ so we will not be like ships tossed about by the winds of doubt (James 1:6). *Hei* is God's open window that will pierce the darkness of these storms and shine on us no matter how dark things may seem.

Hei's Song of Strength

I want to tie together everything we have learned about *hei* and show you just how beautiful these word pictures can be. I want you to *behold* how valuable you are to God and how His Spirit hovers over you to mark you as His.

God's chosen people, the Hebrews, were established when God changed the names of Abram and Sara to Abra*h*am and Sara*h*. Scholars suggest Abram's Mesopotamian name, meaning lofty father, related to the gods of the moon-worshipping society he came from in ancient Babylonia. Likewise, Sara appears to relate to the Mesopotamian moon goddess of Ur. *Elohim* desired to mark Abram and Sara with their new identity and separate them from their previous lives. When God breathed *hei* into their names and marked them as His, He established Abraham as the father of multitudes, a covenant promise only fulfilled by *Elohim*. Today, when we choose to accept the gift of salvation by recognizing the crucifixion and resurrection of Jesus, He sends His Spirit, *hei*, to mark and seal those who are His forever (Ephesians 1:13).

Most Bible versions translate 2 Timothy 3:16 as God's Word being *inspired*. The Greek word for *inspired* is *theopneustos*, and it is a combination of two root words, *Theo* meaning God, and *pneu*, which means to blow or breath. God created the world, gave life to man, and shared His Word with us by His very breath. Strong woman, you are a child of the King, and you are loved and valued. The God of heaven desires to bless you with every good and perfect gift and extend His benefits to you. Let everything that has breath praise the Lord (Psalm 150:6). Breathe His name. Know you can face the world and filter what is thrown at you as He propels you forward by His Holy Spirit. Behold, He is hovering over you.

After her divorce, Joy only embraced her new identity with Christ's help. Through their time of healing, her family recognized God's intentional care and faithfulness toward them. As they moved to a new area for a fresh start, she asked her children to pray for their new home. One evening her young son sweetly confessed that he had not been praying for a new house but instead had been asking God for a creek to play in. "God was so faithful. He loves and cares for little boys who just want to play in creeks with frogs. Earlier that very day my realtor showed me a house with a creek in the backyard. God used my son to confirm in my heart it was to be our home." Another time, her daughter asked for new shoes. They were completely outside of their budget. Almost as a joke, Joy encouraged her daughter to pray for them. "A friend invited my daughter to a garage sale, and she returned with those exact shoes in the color she wanted. They only cost her two dollars. Those innocent prayers bolstered our prayer life. We began watching how the Lord became our father, provider, and sustainer." What prayers has God answered for you lately? Even His smallest provision is worth celebrating.

Joy is now remarried, and her new husband is a pastor who had never married and didn't have kids. He adopted Joy's children. God's providence provided the children with a father who was also adopted as a child because he too was abandoned. Isn't that what Jesus does for us? He adopts us into His family so we too can learn the steady security of a father's love. Today Joy is an author and speaker at women's conferences with a heart for single moms. "There is such power in perspective. Single moms see their situation through their viewpoint, and it can be blurred. There is hope when we filter our circumstances through God's perspective. When we behold Him as our husband, our shepherd, and our leader, we begin to see Him as our provider." What does your perspective on life reveal? You too can be moved by the Holy Spirit and behold God's provision in your life. Jesus desires to be your beloved. He peers through the window's lattice and watches you with love (Song of Solomon 2:9). He is eager to come into your presence and breathe new life into you.

Pause and Reflect—Discussion Questions

1. Society's definition of sin changes constantly. What behavior is accepted today that even just a few years ago would have been called what it is: sin?

_____

_____

_____

_____

_____

2. How does society's acceptance of this sin affect your family?

_____

_____

_____

_____

_____

3. How do you filter what society has to offer before it enters your home?

_____

_____

_____

_____

_____

4. When a doctor listens to our lungs with a stethoscope he asks us to take a deep breath. Do that now. Take a deep breath like you would for your doctor. Exhale. Did you hear it? Did you say YHWH? How does it feel to know the very breath that sustains your life also speaks the holy name of God? Every breath!

_____

_____

_____

_____

_____

Praying the *Alef-Bet*

Holy Lord, Your very breath sustains my life, and the breath of Your Spirit marks me as Yours. Holy Spirit, tether me to Your leadings, and reveal Your truth to me so I will behold Your blessings in all aspects of my life. Lord, help me filter through all I am faced with, and strengthen me as I live to reflect Your holiness. Amen.

ו

She Is Attached to Christ

Vav—the Nail

Proverbs 31:15

The sixth letter of the Hebrew alphabet is *vav*, with the word picture of a nail. It refers to binding and securing. *Vav* is a prefix used to indicate a transition of time, past, present, and future. *Vav* is also the conjunction *and*. It reveals the connection between heaven *and* earth, the spiritual *and* physical worlds. In English, we might cringe at using *and* to begin a sentence, but in Hebrew, it is perfectly acceptable. "The *vav* links words and phrases to form sentences; it joins sentences into paragraphs and chapters . . . The absence of a [*vav*] at the beginning of a new chapter in the Torah indicates the beginning of a new era or subject."[1]

Vav is the connecting *and* in Proverbs 31:15 as the memory trigger. The concluding thought of verse 14, "She brings her food from afar," is joined to verse 15, "[*and*] she rises also while it is still night." Her actions are continuing from one verse to another. Let's explore this a bit more.

---

1. Rabbi Michael L. Munk, *The Wisdom in the Hebrew Alphabet: The Sacred Letters as a Guide to Jewish Deed and Thought* (Brooklyn, NY: Mesorah Publications Ltd., 1983), 95.

And She Rises Also While It Is Still Night

In verse 14 the strong woman brings a variety of options for her family. She wisely filters her offerings, *and* she begins before the break of day. Most Jewish commentaries recognize the Proverbs 31 Woman as one who invests her whole heart into everything she does. She will not rest until her job is complete, even if it requires her to rise while it is still dark and first attach herself to the heart of God.

The Hebrew word for night is *layil*. It means to twist or fold away and contains the idea that as our day comes to an end, God folds up and tucks away the sunlight, leaving us the night. Darkness is often a symbol of sin or evil. We may be tempted to hide in the dark because it protects us from seeing the reality of our lives. Proverbs encourages us to filter through the world's offerings, but darkness can distort our view.

Stacey is a firecracker. Her energy is relentless, with a can-do attitude and a servant's heart. If you met her today, you would see Proverbs 31 written all over her. Stacey understands how darkness distorts our view. Married four times, she attached herself to the wrong men. With this past, how can she be a Proverbs 31 Woman? Stacey will tell you she has had four marriages but only one husband. When they met in the ninth grade, he knew she was it for him, except it took nearly thirty years to convince Stacey. Together they have overcome the prevailing darkness in their lives.

I often awake well before sunrise. When my mind is swirling with worry and responsibility, this early wake-up tends to make me restless. Even Jesus experienced restlessness as He faced His darkest hours. From His early morning prayers, I see the importance of using the quiet morning hours as a time to pray and seek God's peace. Like the Proverbs 31 Woman, you may have to rise while it is still dark in order to listen for His voice. Savor the quiet of a prayerful, early morning, knowing He faces the darkness with you. Is it hard for you to tuck away the day's worries? Christ alone is your connection to God's security and peace. When we attach our minds to God's truth, rather than our circumstances and feelings, we can look forward to a new day unfolding.

And Gives Food to Her Household

Stacey attended a Catholic church growing up. She sang the children's songs and heard the stories, but a relationship with God remained unexplored. The experiences left her with the feeling that "God was approached through a trail of bodies. I had to get through my parents' approval, the saints, a priest, then maybe God would listen. Eventually, the struggles I faced wrapped around my heart and choked out my faith in Christ." Nails of disappointments and poor decisions were driven deep into her confidence, sealing away any hope of ever measuring up to women like the Proverbs 31 Woman. Stacey attached herself to one man, then another, and another. Providing for her daughters was her top priority, but her offerings did not include sustaining food presented from God's banquet table.

The word *food* in verse 15 is the Hebrew word *terep*. It is primarily translated as "food," but I encountered one use, which suggests the Proverbs woman is fierce. Commentator Michael V. Fox describes *food* like this: "The word's predominant meaning, 'prey,' 'plunder,' gives it overtones of aggression and pugnacity, as if to hint that the woman of strength is something of a lioness in providing for her young."[2] Combine this definition with the understanding that a woman of strength doesn't stop until she completes her task, and we can appreciate how purposeful she is. When it comes to defending my young, I easily relate to the momma bear. But providing like a lioness means I'm stealthy, patient, and calculating. I will relentlessly chase down what is needed. Not to acquire more but to be purposeful with my time and resources. I filter

---

2. Michael V. Fox, *Proverbs 10–31: A New Translation with Introduction and Commentary,* The Anchor Yale Bible, vol. 18B (New Haven: Yale University Press, 2009), 894.

through what is offered to my family, *and* when I recognize something essential and worthy for God, it becomes a valuable resource like the spoils of victory because it was fiercely vetted. How easy is it for you to recognize God's resources? You work hard to provide. Are you offering quality over quantity? How do you plunder His resources?

The strong woman feeds her family spiritual meat, not junk food, and rests only when her job is done. To keep this task from turning into an unattainable to-do, remember the necessity of attaching yourself, like a nail, to the strength and guidance of Christ. He is what makes you strong, even as you rise out of the darkness, which metaphorically can include your struggles and conflicts. The flow of the poem shows the Proverbs woman rises *and* prepares spiritual nourishment *and* portions it to her household. How can you be the connecting *vav* between God *and* your family? What spiritual nourishment can you offer? Are you able to receive the meat of a relationship with Christ, or are you still drinking milk (Hebrews 5:12)?

Stacey has encountered many *vavs* of connection in her life. One woman with whom she worked was very open about her faith and relationship with Jesus. "The actions of her faith and her warrior prayers spoke volumes. She told me often that Jesus wanted an active relationship with me, not just knowledge of Him. Finally, because of her example, after years of keeping my back turned to Christ, I was ready to face Him."

Desperation and weariness hung from her like rags, but Stacey summoned her last ounce of bravery and returned to church. That first sermon began stripping away those rags of defeat. She encountered Jesus as never before. "The Pastor was doing a series about our position in Christ, what a godly life looks like, marriage, parenting, everything I needed to hear! I had so many questions. I had never heard *this* Jesus before. My coworker fostered a personal connection with me and reconnected me to the God who fiercely loved and pursued me regardless of my past."

Stacey courageously questioned all she learned. "Rather than being judgmental, my new friends were patient with me. They answered my questions and helped me mature as a Christian." Her tribe poured into her for years and helped to secure her relationship with Christ. That sweet boy from ninth grade, with whom she maintained a lifelong friendship, began noticing a difference in her.

Like Stacey, he too faced insurmountable obstacles life sometimes requires. At one point he attempted suicide, but Stacey doggedly maintained their friendship and continued to share the difference Christ made in her life. Hope bloomed the day he mentioned his desire to have what Stacey had. She wisely recognized an opportunity to connect him to her Savior. She responded, "Can I introduce you to my God? Not the one you think you know but a God of the peace we desperately need in life." Their hearts knit together through a relationship with Christ, and they eventually married. The deep scars etched into their hearts from a lifetime of conflict began to smooth. Stacey joyfully added, "The church responded in love, and through their response, my husband was able to see the love of Christ through someone other than me. He understood Christ's unconditional love because he experienced it through all of us first-hand." Who have you connected to Christ? Perhaps your child, a friend, or a family member? One of the blessings of heaven will be seeing how I played a part in someone's salvation.

And Portions to Her Maidens

The Hebrew word for portion here is *hoq,* which is usually a reference to the mistress giving portion and orders to her maidservants. The context implies a fixed appointment of time and quantity, but it's more than a serving size. Some suggest the verse reveals a contrast between the household members who will receive an unlimited portion of her time while others outside of her home will receive a fixed amount.

A lesson for us might be that we are to be unlimited in our love, time, and attention to our family. However, for others, we are to be more inclined to allot a fixed portion. This makes me wonder how often I seek God's guidance in portioning my time. My best use of time is helping others nail down their spiritual need and portion to them the plunder, the meat of my relationship with Christ.

An old Aesop fable might help you relate. There was once a miser who buried his treasure in a field. He visited it daily to count and admire it, but he always reburied the treasure and left it hidden. One day a thief, after watching him, snuck in to steal the treasure. When the miser discovered his cache was missing, he cried out in distress. A passerby asked why he didn't just use the wealth, but the miser wailed that he would never spend such a treasure. In response, the stranger tossed him a rock and told him to bury it, because it had the same value as his lost treasure. This fable is like the parable of the talents mentioned in Matthew 25.

The treasure we offer includes our life experiences, talents, spiritual gifts, faith, and our time. It's the *and* in our lives. Like the miser in the fable, spending our treasure requires risk and nerve. Or, like the lioness, patience and stealth. God grants us this gift of life—yes, the good, the bad, even the messy—so we can share it with others *and* impact His kingdom.

A nail, once driven into wood with great force, will over time become loose, and the connection will weaken. You only need to walk across a wooden floor and encounter a squeak to know the nail has separated from the foundational subfloor. The joints require maintenance so the connection doesn't become useless. We need to be set firmly into *our* foundation as well. We face big challenges in life. We need a big nail, like ones that set a railroad track or hung our Savior from a cross. As we provide others with a portion of our God-given treasure, it is essential that we receive our daily portion from God. How do you receive His portion for you? Deuteronomy 6:6–8 tells us to bind His Word to us. The word bind, *qashar,* in Deuteronomy can also be translated as "gird," "strengthen," and "reinforce." Some lexicons add an interesting note to its definition in that *qashar* can also mean to be joined together mentally in love. A nail bound Jesus to a cross so I would be connected to His love, which is reinforced by reading His Word—a never-ending cycle of strength.

Vav's Song of Strength

Exodus 27:9–10 describes the tapestry curtains of the Tabernacle hanging from hooks, or in Hebrew, *vavs.* Images of heavenly angels were woven into the linen curtains to serve as a daily reminder of the Tabernacle's identity, the connection between heaven and earth. What have you nailed to yourself as your identity? Does shame or inadequacy hang from you like a worn curtain from a hook? Or perhaps you can drape across yourself confidence and bravery. If so, you are in the minority. Most of us are defeated by the lies we shroud ourselves with. *Vav* holds encouragement to remove the binding rags that hang from us. Focus on the fact Christ offers us the white linen of a new identity, which includes forgiveness, redemption, restoration, and healing.

Like Stacey, I traded in those rags for linen befitting the Tabernacle. As a teenager, I was raped by a boy I trusted to give me a ride home from school on an afternoon like so many others in Florida, filled with torrential thunderstorms. Little did I know he would take me to his house and refuse to bring me home, unless . . . For a long time, I draped myself with shame, weakness, and blame. But the shame wasn't mine. Oh, I was expert in blaming myself. I should have walked home in the rain. I could have stayed in the car. If I really didn't want it to happen, I would have fought harder. I shoulda, coulda, woulda. But the shame wasn't mine. It belongs to the boy who took advantage of a situation and improperly used his position of power. I don't have to wear the shame. The shame is his to wrestle with.

The Bible offered me a new identity when I became a follower of Christ. Ephesians 4:24 tells me to "put on the new self, which in *the likeness of* God, has been created in righteousness and holiness of the truth." This new self is renewed according to the image of the One who created me (Colossians 3:10). Jesus knows how it feels to have men wield their power and take advantage of the weak. I wear His image with pride. I'm sad those events happened to me, but I choose to connect myself to the God who loves me, and I do not drape myself with shame.

I forgive the boy who abused me. I'll be honest; my heart doesn't bubble with love for him, but I have deep peace. When the memories of that event threaten to plague me, I do not give the shoulda, coulda, woulda victory. Instead, I pray for that boy who's now a man. I pray for his repentance, so he can encounter Christ. Take off your grave clothes. Christ walks with us out of any darkness holding us back. When we nail our doubt, sin, and pain to Christ, it is crucified with Him (Galatians 2:20). This foundational belief becomes essential as we look at the next lesson of Proverbs 31 in verses 16, 17, and 18. The military theme will continue as we see how a strong woman faces spiritual warfare.

Pause and Reflect—Discussion Questions

1. Who do you usually connect with when you need encouragement?

_____

_____

_____

_____

2. Consider all that you do. How well do you portion your time?

_____

_____

_____

_____

3. What curtains do you feel are draped over you and define you?

_____

_____

_____

_____

4. If you are comfortable, share when you nailed down your relationship with Christ and all doubt of your salvation was removed.

_____

_____

_____

_____

Praying the *Alef-Bet*

Lord Jesus, thank You for being my *vav*, my connection to salvation.
Because of Your sacrifice for me, sin no longer hangs from me. Instead,
I can attach to myself a newness that only You offer. Thank You for
walking me through the darkness. I pray You will strengthen me to
portion my time wisely so I can consistently provide spiritual nourishment for others.

She Wields the Word of God

Zayin—the Weapon

PROVERBS 31:16

The mission field was not what Kellye expected. Each morning from her kitchen window, she looked over a neighborhood filled with people she was expected to interact with. Her family hoped to introduce them to Christ. Brutal honesty revealed she didn't like them. Overwhelming darkness shrouded this Eastern European city both physically and metaphorically. It was slowly suffocating her daughter and made her family's life grim.

What do the following words have in common—seed, lightning bolt, protection, strength, and gossip? If said in Hebrew, they all contain the letter *zayin* and an essence of power derived from *zayin's* word picture, a weapon. Look at the letter. Can you recognize the sword's hilt and body?

Zayin also represents the number seven. If we trace the biblical generations, we discover man's first encounter with iron was in the seventh generation. Genesis 4 confirms Tubal-cain forged bronze and iron and formed the first swords. We use weapons to attack or defend. Consider this interesting Hebrew wordplay. *Zayin* is a root letter in the words *stranger* and *enemy*. The pictures of both words relate to a man of weapon. When confronted by enemies wielding weapons, it helps to have one as well. *Zayin* is the weapon. The enemy we face is crafty and unrelenting. The strong woman recognizes this threat and prepares for battle.

Safely cocooned in her church's traditions of friendship and fellowship, Kellye moved easily within the Christian community. That is until betrayal cut her idyllic understandings to the core. She felt shunned from people she counted as friends, and the experience caused a deep questioning in her understanding of church membership. She adds, "I expected Christians to treat each other differently, but some displayed a very worldly response. I found myself hesitant to trust Christian women again. Our family became isolated, and our prayers contained a longing to know if there was more to the church and the Christian life. Our hearts hungered for God's will, and He honored our prayers." Can you relate to Kellye's pain? Has the church hurt you? It can be hard to separate the body of Christ as a whole from individuals who misrepresent Christ and overreach their perceived responsibilities. How have you responded?

As Kellye sought God's leading, He planted the idea of missionary work in her heart. She didn't mention this to her husband until the spark of an idea fanned into an uncontainable consuming fire. "We sat at dinner one night and I blurted out, 'We need to consider missions work. I think we have to go overseas.'" As though holding his breath, her husband exhaled and asked, "What do you think of Eastern Europe?" Unknown to the other, each had prayed about entering the mission field for months. His response and the city he identified immediately confirmed their similar prayers. They tested every decision like Gideon's fleece (see Judges 6:36–40). "If at any time we received a no, we took it as our misunderstanding of God's call, but He kept unfolding His plans for us."

She Considers a Field and Buys It

Proverbs 31:16 introduces a new topic for the strong woman. Her investment into her home has gained fruit. The Hebrew words in this verse will deepen our understanding. The strong woman considers or evaluates a new field. Consider, or *zamam,* זָמַם, is the memory trigger beginning with *zayin.* The word implies a first look to identify what might prevent growth in her investment, and she plans. Like a military warrior, she does reconnaissance work before purchasing the land to ensure the quality of her vineyard, or garden.

Some translations add she purchases the field with her gains or profit. The word is *priy,* the fruit of her labor. It indicates her productivity. This investment requires time to prune and cultivate, and she calculates the cost. Christians are encouraged to be fruitful, but do we consider the soil in which we plant ourselves? A strong woman does, and she evaluates how best, and in what soil, she continues to bear the fruit.

Kellye continues, "My husband thrived on the mission field, but it cost us dearly. It was difficult. In America, I worked outside of the home, at the top of my field as an educator. In Russia, I became a stay-at-home mother who homeschooled. I barely cooked, and there were no brownie mixes to be found in the entire country. To top it off, I couldn't even communicate with a toddler!"

Their teenage daughter struggled the most. During language lessons they often heard from another room the slow, steady thud of her head hitting the side of a dresser in frustration. "It was the most difficult parenting time of my life. Our daughter would sob, 'Jesus doesn't have a plan for my life. If He did, He wouldn't put me somewhere I'm so unhappy.' I was convinced within the first year to return home. How could I justify this child who was floundering?"

One goal they had was to engage the Chuvash people group with the gospel. "No evangelical had ever contacted this group. They had zero knowledge of Christ, and we did not speak their language. We offered

English lessons in our home, and only two people showed up. We were convinced we were the worst missionaries ever. But a young man with broken English who joined our group made his introductions by simply saying, 'I am Chuvash.' The room became silent. We knew we were amid God's moving. Through him, we established a relationship with his village."

As their group continued to reach out to the Chuvash, Kellye's daughter had an opportunity to help with translating. The experienced catapulted her passion for missions. "Once my daughter discovered her purpose for suffering, she could endure. Today, she never looks at anything from her life as 'that time God did *to* me' but instead as 'that time God did *for* me.'" Have you, like Kellye, faced a time when you felt as though you were bumbling through God's plan? Or worse, failing Him? How does knowing this may be part of God's plan change your perspective? The good, bad, and ugly can all be used by Him.

I've never lived in a foreign country like Kellye, but I've relocated cities. My biggest obstacle was finding a new church or deciding which little league team my son would play on. Nothing like the soil-testing Kellye faced. So often I quit when things became hard, but Kellye's story makes me question if I missed a life-changing blessing or a lesson.

In Matthew 13:44, Jesus describes a man who discovered a field containing a treasure. Like Kellye and the Proverbs woman, the man invested everything into the field. Treasure is often found only through the hard work of mining and digging. How do you embrace the change when God replants you? Do you allow God's plan to take root and grow, or do you let the ground turn fallow? What treasure have you found in the fields God has planted you?

From Her Earnings She Plants a Vineyard

Zayin emphasizes the military theme and stresses women can be valiant warriors who wield their weapons defensively. Let's consider another Hebrew word containing the letter *zayin*. The word *oz* means mighty, force, strength, and fortress. Psalm 46:1 describes God as "our refuge and strength [*oz*], a very present help in trouble." It's translated "strength" but can read, "God is our mighty force." Is this a promise you cling to when facing adversity?

Oz is a root word in the word *ezer*, which means a mighty force that is a help. It is usually a reference to the might of God or His armies. Look at the following verses.

> Daniel 10:13: Michael, one of the chief princes, came to help [*ezer*]
> me.
> Joshua 1:14: You shall cross before your brothers in battle array,
> all your valiant warriors, and shall help [*ezer*] them.
> Psalm 70:5: Hasten to me, O God! You are my help [*ezer*] and my
> deliverer.

Genesis 2:18 names Eve as Adam's suitable helper. She was created to be his *ezer*, his helping force. One commentary renders the translated phrase "helpmeet, *ezer*, for him," as help in front, one who goes before. We're talking about someone who is "a far cry from the traditional view of a woman's role as 'the little helper.' . . . We're talking here about a tough, Green Beret, Special Forces kind of woman!"[1] It makes sense that Satan tempted Eve before Adam. If he could breach her guarding force, he had full access to his primary target. Consider this. When a

Let me share another commentary about our value as *ezer*. "The wife's function is to guard and defend her husband. Only with her help can he stand against the forces of Satan, the powers that scheme to overthrow him. [Jewish] Sages explain that God . . . created woman [as] man's weapon of defense, against the Accuser."[2] It makes sense that Satan tempted Eve before Adam. If he could breach her guarding force, he had full access to his primary target. Consider this. When a

---

1. Pat Mercer Hutchens, *Hebrew for the Goyim: Bible Codes* (Maitland, FL: Xulon Press, 2007), 71.
2. Glazerson, *Building Blocks of the Soul*, 108.

king conquered a city, his forces preceded him as he marched in and took possession. The king was still the leader, but the strength and help that went before him is *ezer*. Married women are this to our husbands. We go before God's throne in intercession so our men can take their rightful positions and lead our family. This thought does not contradict the spiritual leadership of men but emphasizes the value of a strong woman as his partner. Eve was created from Adam's side. When men and women are joined in marriage the two sides become whole, and each provide needed help, strength, and support.

Kellye faced subtle spiritual battles not easily detected. "It began as criticism and self-defeating thoughts. I didn't classify it then as spiritual warfare, but looking back I see it clearly. My emotions were my biggest weakness, and Satan used them against me. Emotions can deceive. It took time, but I learned to stop the defeating thoughts." Living as missionaries in Eastern Europe presented other spiritual battles and risks. At one point the government took her family's passports. Kellye adds, "This was very dangerous. When on the streets, we told the kids not to look anyone in the eye. If approached, they were to pretend they did not speak the language. We had to find a balance with our children between honestly saying we did not know what would happen to us and not frightening them. We lived in a dark place, metaphorically and spiritually. Some of the situations we faced were terrifying, but we learned through the difficulties and grew."

When reassigned to another country, Kellye's family helped establish a church. During a forty-five-minute trek home after an especially long opening day, their daughter commented, "That was the longest, hardest day, but it was the best day ever." Satan goes to great effort to hold back, destroy, and rob the joy of God's people. We can overestimate or underestimate his power, which hinders our influence. The Bible describes him as a prowling lion seeking to devour us (1 Peter 5:8). He must stand before the throne of God and ask permission to sift us, but God is sovereign. Kellye adds, "That church is thriving today.

Those hard moments make me grateful. He knows our fight, and He is trustworthy." Did you catch that? Kellye was grateful for the battle. In the heat of your skirmish, are you ever grateful?

Our prayers are equipped with an arsenal of God's power, especially when we pray His Word and do the most unlikely—praise Him. His sword of the Spirit (Ephesians 6:17) is your offensive weapon. The Greek word for sword in Ephesians 6:17 is *máchaira*. Would it surprise you to know this is a small dagger used in hand-to-hand, up close and personal combat? Hebrews 4:12 describes it as a living, sharp, double-edged sword. The Proverbs 31 Woman is not afraid of fierce prayer. She also responds in praise. Second Chronicles 20 describes the Israelites praising God as they marched in to battle because God promised to be with them and go before them. Their praise was their weapon. The sword of strength in God's Word, prayer, and our praise will pull down strongholds. They help us take every thought captive and make it obedient to Christ (2 Corinthians 10:4–6). They help us to be strong and courageous (Joshua 1:8–9) as no weapon formed against us will prosper (Isaiah 54:17). Our sword is double edge, but we cannot be double-minded toward our trust in Christ.

Kelley spent quiet mornings in her kitchen overlooking her city. "Before I understood spiritual battles, my quite time was more like a to-do list. I'm a rule follower. I was told to have a quiet time, so I checked it off. But in that kitchen, with clenched teeth, I prayed for people I didn't like and read five psalms a day. I read the whole book once a month. God embraced my anger. He is a big God; He can handle it. I not only prayed 'How long, Lord?' (Psalm 13), but also, 'You have set my feet' (Psalm 31:8). My prayers changed. In time, I wanted every person in that city, as far as I could see, to experience the love of God as I did." There is power when we speak the name of Jesus. His name is above all rule, authority, dominion, and name (Ephesians 1:21). When we trust in His name, we can face the multitudes.

Zayin's Song of Strength

The type of soil you plant a vineyard in is just as important as the type of grape you plant. The field's preparation determines the fruit's production. Dry soil produces small grapes rich in flavor. Soil damp with excess rain produces plump grapes, but the flavor may be diluted. The vinedresser continuously inspects clusters of grapes for mold or decay. Neglecting to prune results in a wild, tangled vine. Vines with no growth are cut away to provide nutrients to the areas that are growing. Each year, the vinedresser must decide whether she will keep the ancient vines producing better-quality grapes, plant new vines, or graph new shoots into the old root system.

Jesus describes Himself as the vine and us as the branches (John 15:5). To ensure we are firmly planted in rich soil and producing the best fruit for His kingdom, we need to take a soil sample. Have you done this? In what activities are you planted? Do your activities or responsibilities require pruning? Prayerfully consider these questions like the strong woman of Proverbs doing reconnaissance work and evaluating her investment.

Psalm 31:21 became a salve to Kellye's soul while serving on the mission field. She clung to the words "Blessed be the LORD, for He has made marvelous His lovingkindness to me in a besieged city." She adds, "He spoke this directly to me in kindness when I was not being kind. He planted us in a besieged city. We were monitored. Our phones and computers were not secure. We kept cash on hand if we had to escape quickly. The government could take us, and we would never be found. Psalm 31:21 confirmed God had not forgotten us. I repeated it anytime I ventured outside of my home." Kellye's trust in God was never diluted. It grew robust in each season as she surrendered to God's gentle pruning. Kellye asks, "How many people have the opportunity to put their lives on the line and know God carried them through?" Are you producing flavorful fruit? Or is it plump and diluted? How is God pruning you? It can seem like a laborious, sometimes painful process, but it is necessary to be part of His healthy, productive vine.

God's pruning trained Kellye's faith and commitment to Jesus. "I trust Him. In our difficulties, we learned to be honest with all of it. Imagine if everyone stopped saying 'it's fine' when things are terrible and instead were honest with God. It is tempting to shine up and gloss over the ugly, but we accept the ugly with the beautiful. Everyone experiences the ugly, and God's power is perfected in our weakness. Just watch Him work. Few rarely volunteer to suffer for Christ, but the process has rubbed some of my hard edges off. I'm grateful God chose to use me."

Pause and Reflect—Discussion Questions

1. How would you describe the fruit you produce? Is it still growing or now mature? How has abiding in Christ helped you?

_____

_____

_____

_____

2. Jesus tells us He will prune branches that do not bear fruit. Describe a time in your life when you felt you were being pruned. How did it help you to be healthy and productive for Him?

_____

_____

_____

_____

3. Think of your activities, responsibilities, and relationships. Your soil is important. Is there anything in your life that needs to be uprooted or replanted?

_____

_____

_____

_____

_____

4. Knowing Satan is actively against us might be unsettling. Can you recall a time of attack? What Bible verses are your defense?

_____

_____

_____

_____

5. Do you tend to overestimate or underestimate Satan's influence? How?

_____

_____

_____

_____

_____

Praying the *Alef-Bet*

Lord, we face incredibly hard battles here on earth. At times we cannot stand without Your strength and protection. As we go before our family, we ask that You filter Satan's attacks and protect us as a mighty force. We thank You for the protective armor offered in Ephesians and Your defensive sword, the Word. Give us wisdom as we invest our time and talents so we will produce worthy fruit for Your kingdom. Help us plant into others with love. Amen

She Prays for a Hedge of Protection

Chet—the Fence or Wall

PROVERBS 31:17

Terri and Brad were married right out of college. Terri was determined to forgo the struggles she faced as a child of divorce, so right from the start, she and her husband began building a marriage with a godly foundation. They attended church, worked in ministry, and surrounded themselves with like-minded friends.

One couple became their best friends. "These were friends we barbecued with and went out with. We did everything together." Her best friend and Brad even worked at the same company. Soon, Terri discovered her husband had an affair with her friend. "It was a one-time event. He was sorry, and he confessed. But how do you start healing when you work with them and go to church with them? You usually have the support of your best friend to help you with something like this. She was my best friend. I was betrayed twice." Terri began to pray.

Chet's word picture is a fence or wall. It is like the letter *hei,* but the window at the top left is closed. Walls have a few purposes. They keep danger out, protect those inside, and define boundaries. Terri's walls of protection were shaky and in desperate need of reinforcement.

Have you considered the types of spiritual battles you face on behalf of your family? Have you prayed fervently for a wayward child or an unfaithful spouse? I have stood with families in a blighted neighborhood who prayed their children would be protected from gun violence. That is a sobering prayer. For some, discouragement after discouragement and loss after loss can seem like a battle. You may have used the phrase "hedge of protection" when praying for yourself and family. This defensive hedge is *chet.*

Just as *hei* related to inhaling breath and the life-giving spirit of God, *chet* is the exhale. The letter is included in words describing a physical activity, labor, or effort that results in a strong exhale. Proverbs 31:17 continues the poem's topic of spiritual warfare. In battle, we need the power of *zayin* and the refuge wall of *chet.* Strong woman, roll up your sleeves and prepare to gird yourself. This will take some effort.

She Girds Herself with Strength

Verse 17 begins with the Hebrew word חָגַר, *chagar*—gird. To gird means to put on around the waist, to gather up. It often relates to strapping a sword around the waist, a sword like *zayin.* It also refers to building a fortified wall around the protected land. Girding and reinforcing is a common theme in the Bible, especially when preparing for war. The Bible describes how God is donned for battle when He fights for us. Psalm 93:1 tells us He is clothed with majesty and is girded with strength. David and his mighty men were men of war. In 2 Samuel 22:40, David acknowledges it is the Lord who girds him with strength for battle. If David, a man after God's heart, girded himself in God's strength, we too can stand firm having girded ourselves with His truth (Ephesians 6:14).

Chet, as the memory trigger, is our reminder to build walls of protection to defend our home and make it a refuge. Several defensive walls are described in the Bible, one being a hedge on every side surrounding Job. Satan references this hedge in Job 1:10 when he spoke before the throne of God. God also instructed Judah to build surrounding walls around their cities so the Lord could give them rest on every side. They did, and they prospered (2 Chronicles 14:7).

When facing her husband's affair, Terri began to understand how intentional Satan is when his target is set. Terri adds, "What a victory it was for the enemy to take out four people and two marriages with one blow. We are all believers, and he took us all out of ministry, destroyed their marriage, and nearly took ours as well. So many times I cried out to God *why?* My husband had a relationship with the Lord. He knew better." One day with the affair long past, Terri felt the Lord impress on her spirit, "The foundation was strong, but your walls were not high enough." This revelation triggered the healing of their marriage, and Terri went to work building through prayer the needed wall.

The Message translation of Proverbs 31:17 paints a determined image of the Proverbs woman.

> First thing in the morning, she dresses for work, rolls up her sleeves, eager to get started.

Each day, in preparation for the difficult battles we might face, we can roll up our sleeves, strap on the Word of God, and seek refuge behind God's protective wall. We have an investment to protect through prayer. Warriors are strengthened through commitment, training, and practice—even prayer warriors. What steps have you taken to strengthen your walls?

Exodus 15:2 tells us the Lord is our strength and song and becomes our salvation. Psalm 59:16 tells us to sing of the Lord's loving-kindness for He has been our stronghold and refuge in the day of our distress. These verses provide an example of the lengths God will go to defend us as we tuck ourselves behind His protection. The Proverbs 31 Woman girds herself with the Lord's strength and stability because she walks with the Lord. I find it interesting that both Psalm 59:16 and Exodus 15:2

refer to singing of God's strength. The psalmist and Moses are telling us to sing a heroic hymn to our Lord. And here, in Proverbs 31:10–31, the Lord inspired a scribe to write a heroic hymn that is still sung over strong women today in recognition of the strength He provides. How has God been your stronghold? What lyrics do you hear Him singing over you?

And Makes Her Arms Strong

You will be happy to know the second half of the verse does not mean you have to hit the gym! The phrase means so much more than working out. Hebrew has more than one word that can be translated as "strong." *Chayil* was one we looked at, and in verse 17, *amats* is another. It primarily means strong, but it can also mean to be alert, mental strength, and to be determined. In having her arms *amats*, the Proverbs woman is so well trained, so fine-tuned her arms have muscle memory. Terri realized she was not as alert as she hoped. She clung to her lifelong verse Psalm 37:25 for comfort and encouragement, which says, "I have been young and now I am old, yet I have not seen the righteous forsaken or his descendants begging bread." Terri is a Proverbs 31 Woman who embraces the teachings of *chet* in Proverbs 31:17. She is a woman of force who wisely inspects the wall of protection for her marriage and family and fortifies any weaknesses she finds through God's Word and as a prayer warrior for her family. We can learn from her. Is there something you need to be more alert to? Do you have a verse or a song you cling to as you gird yourself for the next phase of life?

Some scholars believe Proverbs 31 was an oral poem written during the time the Israelites returned from exile in Babylon to rebuild the walls of Jerusalem. The workers understood their wall was necessary for protection. Half of the workers wore a sword girded to their side while the other half stood guard holding spears (Nehemiah 4:16–18). They worked continuously, alert and prepared for danger as they built a defense for the city and their families. They also stationed defenders behind the exposed places in the wall. This is how we can face the task of defending our family through prayer, and even more so when we are fortified with a prayer partner. We cannot battle alone. We need to build our protective walls high enough to withstand the enemy's attack and seek prayer partners to help us defend our exposed places.

So how does one not only survive the enemy's attack but thrive? Especially an affair? Without skipping a beat, Terri will tell you, "I fell in love with Jesus. I couldn't immediately turn to my husband or anyone else, so I developed a deep intimacy with God." Who is your prayer partner? Who stands with you when facing your biggest struggles? How do you join with others and go before the throne of God? A well-constructed wall is only as strong as its foundation, and that foundation should be none other than Jesus Christ (1 Corinthians 3:11).

Terri adds, "I thought if I followed the rules and checked off the boxes for a godly life my marriage would succeed, and I would be blessed. That was not the case, and I had to love Jesus anyway." Like a fragile, new lamb, Jesus hand-fed her. Terri continues, "A shepherd will hand-feed for two reasons. When he sees something special in the lamb and wants to cultivate it or when it is injured and needs to recover." This same attention is applied to building a wall of protection. Terri focused on the master builder, and He began to rebuild and fortify the new growth in her heart. He hand-fed her as she healed.

Her relationship with Jesus deepened, and it cemented in her a spirit of forgiveness. "I knew how other women dealt with forgiveness, and for me, it had to be all or nothing. I didn't want to revisit this pain and have him apologize every day. We needed to move on. I couldn't have a checklist for him to complete before I could forgive him. If he did this one thing, check, I could forgive. The problem with that is something else always gets added to the list. My forgiveness built from Christ and my love for Christ." And now, twenty-nine years later, they have served Christ together through youth ministry, counseling, and as prayer partners. They have created a retreat center in an old barn they lovingly restored to offer the weary a place of peaceful refuge.

If married, you and your spouse can build the same forgiveness and intimacy as you pray. Because our lives are so busy, we may have to circle a date on the calendar and make an appointment for prayer. Prayer is necessary and worth the effort. As you pray, face each other, join hands, and gently press your foreheads together. You are rebuilding intimacy, vulnerability, and trust. You are supporting each other and softly feeding your souls.

There is never a good time to exhale and completely let our guard down while living in this world. Knowing you have girded yourself in God's truth, His strength, and the knowledge the Messiah is your refuge and foundation does allow you to cease striving (Psalm 46:10) and stand with confidence behind His wall of defense. Only because you have placed your trust in Him. *Chet* reminds you that the refuge and protection of Christ are offered, but you still need to roll up your sleeves, be alert, and stand firm. Prayer is my way of releasing my words to God. Try it. Take a deep breath, then exhale. Your prayers are just like that. We breathe out our words and allow Him to do the physical work of His response. Do this each day and ask God, "Did I miss something today? Is there something I should be watchful for?"

It is okay to fall under His protection and cry out, asking Him to fortify the wall against your enemies. The Israelites faced an insurmountable task of rebuilding the city walls. Every person rolled up their sleeves and participated in the work, including the women. Life can be hard, and the trials are too much for us. Sometimes the enemy does not direct his focus on us but our loved ones. As the enemy rains down his attack, we prepare ourselves to work, but we must also depend on the strength of God's stronghold.

Proverbs 31:16 and 17—Speak firmly to the responsibility of intercessory prayer and girding ourselves with the Word of God and the Sword of the Spirit.

2 Corinthians 10:5—His Word and Spirit help us to take all thoughts captive.

Ephesians 6:18—Strengthened, we can battle against the spiritual forces of wickedness.

You are a woman of strength. Seek Him in prayer and ask Him to fortify your walls with confidence in Him.

Chet's Song of Strength

Jewish scholars suggest the written construction of the letter *chet* is a combination of two letters, *vav* (ו) and *zayin* (ז). Together (ח), the two seem to have a hunchback bridge that appear to hover over them. Scholars suggest this hovering is like the Spirit hovering over void waters of the earth in Genesis 1 just as God exhaled creation. Others believe the hump looks like the marriage canopy, the *chuppah,* used in a Jewish wedding ceremony to represent the spirit of God hovering over the establishment of a new marriage. *Chuppah* begins with the letter *chet.*

When a brand-new home is built, builders can start from scratch and use new materials to create a beautiful, free-of-flaws, never-used home for a family to move into. What happens when someone moves into a dilapidated fixer-upper riddled with foundation problems, crooked walls, and a roof in shambles? It will take significant work to create perfection.[1] We all enter marriage in some form of imperfection. We are never free of flaws. A couple enters the *chuppah* as two individuals but leaves as a unit with the Spirit of God hovering over them. Our homes and family will never wholly resemble perfection because we are

---

1. This analogy appears in Rabbi Aaron L. Raskin, *Letters of Light* (New York: Sichos in English, 2003).

all fixer-uppers. Our restoration is only possible through the grace of God. The hope of our family is built in the presence of God who joins us as we hover over our family in prayer.

If we are to be prayer warriors, we should know what the Word of God suggests we do.

> It tells us to pray eagerly and watch for the Lord (Psalm 5:3).
>
> We are to pray in our heavenly father's name (Matthew 6:9) with thanksgiving and not anxiety (Philippians 4:6).
>
> We are to be devoted to prayer, keeping alert (Colossians 4:2) and praying without ceasing (1 Thessalonians 5:17).
>
> The Bible also promises that in our weakness, His Spirit intercedes for us (Romans 8:26), and the Bible confirms God hears our prayers (Psalm 6:9 and 1 Kings 9:3).
>
> Your prayers are important to God. They are intermingled with fragrant incense burning before God (Revelation 8:4). He will never leave us or forsake us (Hebrews 13:5). But, when we venture outside of His boundaries, we are taking the risk of exposing ourselves to the enemy and creating a weakened area in our wall of defense.

I'd like to finish Terri's story with a resounding, "They lived happily ever after." Their marriage is strong, healthy, and solid. They are both active in ministry and often partner with others in prayer, mentoring, and discipleship. But just as a godly life does not prevent Satan's attack, neither does God's restoration guarantee shelter from future struggles we will face in our fallen world. "All of this has taught me to carefully consider where I invest my time. I love to counsel and walk with those struggling, but I wait for God to reveal His special assignments. I feel that God has used me to point people to the sufficiency of Jesus—no matter their trial."

Consider the importance of prayer and how valuable you are to your family. I want to leave you with a final quote from a commentary offered about Proverbs 31:17 and the strength of the Proverbs 31 Woman:

"A heroic poem for someone engaged in domestic labor is remarkable in the ancient world, and shows something of how God regards the work of women. The great battle of the world is between the seed of the serpent and the seed of the woman [a reference to Genesis 3:15] . . . In their care for their households, wise women are on the front lines of God's holy war. . . . The emphasis [throughout the poem] is on the glory and beauty of the woman's strength, productivity, wisdom, and prudence. Those don't fade."[2]

You are this woman. Stand firm on the frontlines and fully depend on Jesus Christ as the wall, the *chet,* of protection for you and those you pray for. Prayer is serious business and holds great power. Hedge your prayer in Christ. Terri and her husband had to learn how to be partners again, but they continue to celebrate their intimacy with each other and with God. God loves you and wants to experience the same with you.

Pause and Reflect—Discussion Questions

1. How do you see yourself as your family's hedge of protection?

_____

_____

_____

_____

_____

_____

_____

2. Peter Leithart, "Proverbs 31:1–31, Introduction," *Patheos* (blog), May 7, 2011, http://www .firstthings.com/blogs/leithart/2011/05/proverbs-introduction.

2. Where are the places in your family's hedge of protection that need fortified?

_____

_____

_____

_____

_____

_____

_____

3. How do you feel about prayer? Is it hard for you to express your emotions of anger, confusion, or dissatisfaction toward God, or are they an honest part of your prayer life?

_____

_____

_____

_____

_____

_____

_____

Praying the *Alef-Bet*

Lord, I pray the hedge of Your protection surrounding my family is well established with strong, impenetrable walls. Lord, strengthen me to be a faithful prayer warrior, always alert, looking for any weakness that needs Your fortification and protection. Amen.

She Does Reconnaissance Work

Tet—the Snake

PROVERBS 31:18

Verse 18 highlights the strong woman's dedication to work and compliments her sense of industriousness and profitable activities. Word studies reveal this verse is filled with wordplay and parallels the duties of Old Testament priests. Some look at the letter *tet* and see in its shape a twisting snake, while others see an empty vessel with an opening at the top, waiting to be filled. That's quite a difference. *Tet* is a letter of contrast. It is a root letter in the words *good, safe, pure,* and *light.* It is also a root letter in *sin, seduce, adversary, Satan,* and *slaughter.* Do you see the contrast?

She Senses That Her Gain Is Good

In Hebrew, this verse begins with the word taste, *tamah.* Different Bible versions translate this word as "perceives," "sense," and "sees." *Tamah* is our key to *tet's* word picture, and it offers a wordplay on the snake image. A snake perceives its surroundings with a flick of its tongue. It tastes to sense what lies ahead. A valuable sensory skill.

Verse 18 completes the group of verses relating to spiritual warfare and the strong woman's defensive actions. In verse 16 she performs reconnaissance work by seriously considering where she invests and cultivates her fruit. She understands the importance of defending her vineyard with *zayin*, the sword of the Spirit. In verse 17, the strong woman hedges her family with *chet*, a wall of protection. Now in verse 18, she inspects her fruit up close and personal, like *tet,* a snake, to perceives its worth.

At one time in her life, the only seeds Elizabeth was interested in sewing were those producing a party. It seemed college and the sisterhood of Greek life offered so much more than the quiet, small, Midwest town she was from. After college, sunshine, sand between her toes, and a cute boy beaconed her to California with the hopes of a new, exciting life. She adds, "I worked hard and played hard. I was free as a bird and the life of the party, but I had no moral compass. I moved there for a boy but stayed because it was so much fun." Or perhaps she was trying hard to bury something.

In California, Elizabeth worked as a pediatric nurse. Caring for sick children while they battled cancer drained her energy and emotions. She admits, "The sicker those babies became, the more I drank. Looking back now I call that time my wilderness years. Despite being full of life, I now recognize how empty and sad I was." Until one day when a coworker invited her to church. "Growing up, my family attended the 8:15 Sunday morning service without fail. But at home, we never opened the Bible or talked about anything we heard at church, so when I left for college, it was easy to leave church behind too. This new church was different from the type I grew up in. I liked it. In fact, I felt so comfortable that when the pastor asked my opinion of California, I confessed a nagging in my gut that I wasn't supposed to stay. The pastor encouraged me to pray about it and obey the answer. I remember thinking, 'Who do I pray to? Obey what?' I was so confused. Until that very moment it had never dawned on me I could have a relationship with Jesus."

Psalm 34:8 encourages us to taste and see the Lord is good. The word used for *taste* in Psalm 34:8 is the same Hebrew word used in

Proverbs 31:18 for *perceives*. We will only perceive the goodness of the Lord and our fruit for Him when we get up close and personal, face-to-face, and taste test. Similarly, we can only determine the goodness or quality of a situation, activity, and person when we wisely and intimately know with whom or what we are surrounding ourselves and the habits we have developed. During her time in California, Elizabeth did not have a relationship with Jesus, and she did not seek the guidance of the Holy Spirit. Yet she still sensed she was not where she was supposed to be. Can you relate? Can you recall a time when something just didn't sit well with you? How did you respond? How can the Holy Spirit help you taste test your situation?

Her Lamp Does Not Go Out at Night

A strong woman intimately knows the value of her work, and she will do what is required to maintain its value well into the night. The word *night* holds additional wordplay with the snake picture. The word translated "night" is *layil*. It is defined literally as a twisting (as away from the light) and figuratively as adversity. We know darkness can symbolize peril. If we apply the figurative meaning, this verse suggests, "Her lamp does not go out at adversity." Understanding the wordplay helps us recognize why night and darkness often symbolize evil. Unlike evil, which, like a snake, may twist away from the light of God, a strong woman will not. She will ensure her light is not extinguished so evil can't gain a foothold. She regularly tastes and tests her work to see that it is good.

Elizabeth eventually moved back to the Midwest. God became the new voice beaconing her. "One of my patients invited me to church. I didn't understand their praise songs. I kept thinking, 'Who was *this* Jesus, so different from the one I grew up with?' I remember crying through an entire sermon about the prodigal son. I was pulled back again and again until I joined a small group for Bible study. We were discussing the Holy Spirit and the Trinity, and once more, I had no clue what they were talking about. I grew up in church and thought my life was firmly established in biblical teaching. It never dawned on me how much I didn't know." As Elizabeth reviewed her past, she realized markers of Christ's pursuit. Within six months she fully surrendered herself to Christ. She adds, "The timing was interesting as well. I was in the early stages of a relationship with a man who would become my husband. He began attending church with me and had similar stirrings. As a result, we completely change the way we dated. We stopped 'playing house' and started dating again from scratch, even committing ourselves to follow God's standard of purity. My unsaved friends didn't understand; I knew their confusion well. It felt awesome to share the changes in my life and be a testament to the power of God." As you taste test your work, your fruit, and your surroundings, it is imperative to surrender the needed change to God. Otherwise our merchandise, if you will, becomes something we wouldn't want to be inspected under a revealing light.

When Jesus stated He is the light of the world, He was bridging the gap between the Old Testament and the New. He proclaimed this bold statement with the backdrop of the Feast of Sukkot, also known as the Feast of Tabernacles. This feast is celebrated to commemorate God's provision for the Israelites while they wandered the desert. The seven-day feast is finalized with a ceremony enacted in total darkness. The Talmud describes that as the sun set, great crowds filled the Temple in darkness and silence. They carried no form of light. Each of the four corners of the Temple held a giant menorah so large the olive oil lighting receptacle at the top could only be reached by climbing a ladder. At a defining moment, "priests kindled fires on great candelabra, lighting up Jerusalem as if it were the middle of the day."[1] The menorah's

---

1. Menachem Posner, "The Joyous Water-Drawing Ceremony," Chabad.org, accessed June 17, 2019, https://www.chabad.org/library/article_cdo/aid/1971019/jewish/The-Joyous-Water -Drawing-Ceremony.htm.

light immediately dispelled the darkness of the Temple. This event was God's reminder of His presence with the Israelites as He led them by fire through the desert. It symbolized the glory of God, the *Shechinah* glory, descending to dwell in the holy of holies.

The Hebrew word for *lamp* in verse 18 is *nyr*, a word traditionally used to reference the lamps of the Tabernacle. These lamps were to continually burn before the Lord and never be extinguished (Leviticus 24:4; Exodus 27:20). When Proverbs 31:18 notes, "her lamp does not go out at night," it references the responsibilities of the Old Testament priests. "Like the priests, the strong woman keeps the lamp burning perpetually, a light in the night."[2] How would you describe your light? Is it a steady blaze or flickering on the brink of being snuffed out?

As Elizabeth meandered through marriage and motherhood, God's gentle nudge to inspect her offerings lingered. "I looked back and compared my church attendance as a child to my current life. It was shocking to see similarities. My passion for Christ was reflecting a slow fade. Attending church had become enough, and I recognized I was no longer purposefully seeking Christ. I was faced with a choice: seek Jesus or settle. I had tasted the joy of an intimate relationship with Jesus, and I longed for the flavor of His love to linger with me. I trimmed my wick and refueled my lamp."

The strong woman's lamp is also an important reminder for us. We are often told that, as Christians, we are to be the light of the world. Philippians 2:15 is an example. It states our actions amid this crazy world will appear as lights. Matthew 5:14 describes us as the light of the world. Jesus is the Light of the World, and if we walk with Him, we have within us the light of life (John 8:12). Christ shines through us and illuminates this dark world. This is a heavy responsibility. We need to know the difference between a glaring spotlight and a warm, welcoming glow like a lighthouse.

---

2. Leithart, "Proverbs 31:1–31, Introduction."

When we focus on what others are going through rather than ourselves, it's easier to be the light. Put yourself in their shoes. Elizabeth shines her light by being aware. "We get so caught up in our own lives we just don't notice others. God gives me moments to be bold. At times it might seem awkward, but 1 Peter 3:15 reminds me it's a gift because I'm to be prepared to share the hope of Christ at any time. I often offer to pray for people I encounter. No one has ever said no."

The word picture of *tet,* the snake, in this verse, reveals another contrast. Proverbs 31:12 describes the strong woman as doing "good and not evil." Some scholars believe this wording references Eve in the Garden of Eden. Here, it is used again, and *tet* recalls the image of the serpent. However, in this verse, the serpent will not tempt the strong woman. Instead, with the help of Christ within her, she perceives good from evil.

Tet's Song of Strength

A strong woman checks often to ensure she is producing quality fruit for the kingdom of God. She understands this is more than an occasional event. Some of us strive to just survive, and we end up producing fruit of mediocre quality. We are at our weakest when we are weary. It is vital to remain yoked to Christ and be aware of our spiritual maturity and the areas of our lives that need continuous prayer and fortification. In Psalm 139:1 and 23 the psalmist asks God to search him, to know him. As we face the battles of life and attack from the adversary, it is so important to check that we do not depend on our own strength or our walls of defense. Instead, seek the Lord, and invite Him to search you, to reveal any struggles or weaknesses you need to be aware of. Then bring them before Him so He can replace them with gladness and peace (Psalm 4:4–8).

Elizabeth admits, "The realization of my slow fade prompted me to make some changes in my life and rekindle my light. I was hanging on to things because of comfort, but they kept me from moving forward in my faith. I prayed for a mentor and began seeking accountability. I wanted continuous transformation." Are you also seeking continuous transformation? Have you noticed a slow fade in your faith? Becoming stagnant serves as our warning sign that we are not producing quality merchandise. Elizabeth began making changes. "I wake up early every morning for a quiet time with the Lord. My time always gets away during the day; it is always full. When I waited until bedtime, I always fell asleep! Jesus comes before my phone, Facebook, Instagram, and email. Some drink coffee; we can't function in the morning without it. We should feel the same way about our time with Jesus. He should be our caffeine." It seems basic, but it is a choice to pursue Him. God's mercy endures forever. If you recognize a mediocre quality in your offerings, He will not withhold His goodness. We can depend on Him when we grow weary.

First John 4:1 encourages us to test what we expose ourselves to. It states, "Beloved, do not believe every spirit, but test the spirits to see whether they are from God, because many false prophets have gone out into the world." Even Job reminds us to do the same, "For the ear tests words as the palate tastes food" (Job 34:3).

To fully enjoy the abundant bounty of God, we taste and sense the spirit of the teachings we hear. Strong woman, you are attached to Christ (*vav*), and He offers you the power and wisdom of His Word (*zayin*). You can rest in the protection of His refuge (*chet*), but a wise woman, like a snake, also consistently inspects her fruit (*tet*) for quality and contaminants. Don't just sample Christ, taste and see that He is good (Psalm 34:8).

Elizabeth remembers, "I always thought pastors and other believers were smarter than me. But one time a pastor made a statement I just didn't agree with. I went home and dug into Scripture. I found twenty-three verses on the subject, and I returned armed with my questions and God's Word. The pastor kept encouraging me to read this and that book on the subject. Here's the problem: he said *book*. I wanted to know what the Bible said." God used the challenge to convict Elizabeth of the need to check everything she learned. "If you had told me I would one day challenge a pastor, I wouldn't have believed you. This was my first taste of understanding the power and importance of God's discernment." Although valuable, books and devotions do not have the power of God's Holy Word marinating in our hearts. Surprisingly, it is easy for our light to dim when we are under good teaching. We may leave feeling great but can stop short by not asking ourselves, "What is my part of this story? What is my responsibility?" Relationships are two-way, and Proverbs 31:10–18 confirms our part.

- 10 *Alef*—We yoke ourselves to Christ and depend on His strength.
- 11 *Bet*—We invite Him to make His home within our hearts.
- 12 *Gimmel*—We accept His loving-kindness.
- 13 *Dalet*—We enter the world but live set apart for Him.
- 14 *Hei*—We allow His Spirit to guide us.
- 15 *Vav*—We attach ourselves to Him and drape ourselves with His new image.
- 16 *Zayin*—We firmly carry the sword of the Spirit as our defense.
- 17 *Chet*—We gird ourselves with His strength and remain in His refuge.
- 18 *Tet*—We taste, test, and confirm our obedience to Him.

You are strong, you can endure, and you are royalty in His eyes. You are His possession, and He has called you out of the darkness (1 Peter 2:9).

Pause and Reflect—Discussion Questions

1. If you had to make a judgment on the fruit you offer Christ, what do you think the quality of your merchandise would be?

_____

_____

_____

_____

_____

2. How well is your light fueled? Do you consistently have a time of prayer, meditation, and reading His Word? If not, how can you improve?

_____

_____

_____

_____

_____

3. How easily do you recognize times when your light is likely to be snuffed out?

_____

_____

_____

_____

_____

4. Do you ask God to search you? Why or why not?

_____

_____

_____

_____

_____

Praying the *Alef-Bet*

Search me, oh Lord, and know my heart. Test me and know my anxious thoughts (Psalm 139:23). Lord, help me reflect Your goodness so others are drawn to You. God, prompt me when Your light in me begins to flicker and I need to pause, rest, and draw again from You. Dispel the darkness from my life. Lord, remind me to taste and see that You are good and know well Your love for me is bountiful, never to be extinguished. Amen.

She Extends Her Hand of Authority

Yud—the Hand

PROVERBS 31:19

P oor, high school dropout, unwed mother. Words are like yarn, pulled from a skein that will never return to its neat form. Instead, they lay in an unraveled heap. Or worse, they are wound tighter and tighter, hiding frayed ends. Words never used to describe the Proverbs 31 Woman. Words overcome by an open hand offering a step up, not a handout.

The next group of verses, Proverbs 31:19–22, introduce the work of the strong woman's hands. *Yud* is the smallest of the Hebrew letters, not much bigger than an apostrophe. Jesus referred to it in Matthew 5:18 when He said, "Not the smallest letter [*yud*] or stroke shall pass from the Law until all is accomplished." The word picture for *yud* is a hand and includes the forearm. It denotes power and possession.

Yud as a suffix indicates ownership. For example, when *yud* (hand) is added to *bet* (house) then ownership of a house has been identified. The imagery is my hand, my house. Consider how we introduce ourselves. We extend our hand. "The ancients believed your heart was in the palm of your right hand. It was your hand that you performed physical labor, it was your hand that you extended to help another, your strength and power were manifested in your hand. Thus a handshake in ancient times was far more than the meeting of fingers, it was the sharing of one's heart."[1] *Yud* may be small, but it is mighty.

Pause here and prayerfully consider your new understanding of *yud* and the importance of God's hand of power and authority. Ask God to remind you of times His hand of possession held you tightly to His heart and when His hand of authority empowered you.

She Stretches Out Her Hands to the Distaff

Yud begins this verse in the word hand, *yad*. The poem describes the strong woman completing her daily work at home. Then, with her hands of authority and service, she interacts with her family and the world. Her hand is reaching for, or is sent out, to the spindle. Biblically, an outstretched hand has a military connotation. For example, Exodus 8 and 9 provide a list of God's power and authority demonstrated through the outstretched hand Moses held against Egypt.

The Proverbs woman's hands work with the same power and authority. "The spinning of textiles was a time-consuming chore. It could be delegated to servants, female or male. The fact that this well-to-do woman performs it is evidence of special industriousness."[2] She willingly assisted her family and acted with authority. Some consider the spindle the shank of the distaff, also known as a whorl in weaving. Like an orchestra conductor's baton, it directs yarn. The authority of her hand reaches out and directs the function of her family. When led by God, one of the smallest parts of the body, *yud,* holds a great deal of authority and influence. How do you influence others? As you

1. Bentorah, *Hebrew Word Study*, 105.
2. Fox, *Proverbs 10–31*, 895.

manage your home, volunteer, or are in the workplace, how does God's authority direct you?

Lisa learned her work ethic at a young age. Her father died when she was two, laying the burden of raising five children squarely on her mom's shoulders. Her mother eventually remarried, but abuse loomed over their family like an ominous cloud. To escape their home's violence, Lisa and her sister often played at a local park. One day they met a couple who would weave hope into Lisa's heart. "They embraced me like a daughter. They mentored me, exposed me to beautiful homes and the arts—things I had never experienced. But I always returned home with the possibility of abuse or another eviction. My life's tapestry began, and I knew there was more in life."

Most tapestries have one side intricately stitched with care while the other reveals a jumble of knots and thread. Lisa's tapestry was the same. At eighteen she faced the tangles of being an unwed mother. Like her mother, she too felt the sting of an abusive relationship. "As much as I didn't want to be with him, I did. He abused me, but at the same time he protected me and stood up to my stepfather." Lisa's mentors offered to care for her baby, but Lisa was committed to keeping her child. Her son became a catalyst for change in her life. When Lisa's mother eventually divorced, her family was determined to stay off welfare. Together they worked hard to support each other. "Mom helped me with the baby, and I helped with the bills. Somehow we managed." But too often they could not make ends meet, and eviction notices chased them from one home to the next.

Spindle, in Proverbs 31:19, reflects the importance of a strong woman. Some extra-biblical linguists have traced the origins of this word. It references a weaving tool, and in some cultures, the structure of the word contains a relation to skill. If this is the case, the verse reads, *she extends her hand to direct her skill.* This emphasizes the value of a strong woman as she extends her hands to offer her knowledge and skill.

God began to unfold His plans for Lisa. "My sister and I would often watch some of the local boys play football at our park. One afternoon I noticed one boy who wasn't a regular. We began talking, and our conversation lasted for hours. We've been together ever since." He loves her well. He was, and still is, her best friend, and he adopted her son. He believed in Jesus Christ and wove the message of Christ's redemption into Lisa's life. They added three more boys to their family and have dedicated their lives to the Lord. "I was able to stay at home for most of their youth. As our lives ebbed and flowed, we homeschooled, and at times I worked. For a season, we both served in the military, but the priority was raising our sons for the Lord.

"At one point I started a cleaning business. I could do this on the side and still have the boys with me." A landlord she worked for recognized something different in Lisa. "He kept encouraging me to get my real estate license. I was a high school dropout who finished with my GED. I never felt worthy of anything more than hard work because of the instability in my childhood home." God graciously blessed her when the landlord-turned-benefactor sent her to school. "It was one of the best real estate schools in the country—like going to Harvard. By studying with them, I qualified to take the real estate test in any state. My first commission check was for $8,600, the largest amount ever seen in a check made out to me."

Lisa's tapestry is filled with color, texture, and shading. Others not only recognized her value but extended their open hands and wove into her heart, adding to her worth. As a young mother and new Christian, she purposed to direct her children toward Christ and instilled an understanding that work is for the Lord. Her family's maxim became, "All that we have is from Him and for His use." How have others extended their helpful hands of authority to assist you? Or perhaps you have had the of joy weaving into others' lives. God will manifest His power through your hand. How can you extend it to others?

And Her Hands Grasp the Spindle

In Hebrew, the second half of the verse doesn't end with spindle. The word isn't there. It ends referencing her cupped hand, *kaf,* the next letter. Her hand cups the spindle, the tool that creates the fabric of her family's life. How does your hand hold your family like the Proverbs woman? What tools have you used to support and direct them? Your tools could be anything, including a degree, counseling, and mentors. Of course, the Bible is our ultimate tool. Deuteronomy 11:22 tells us to hold fast to God. When we stumble and hurdle forward, we do not need to fear; we grasp the hope set before us (Hebrews 6:18) so we can ultimately embrace eternal life (1 Timothy 6:12). These are all tools we can use to direct our family.

When Lisa compares where she came from with the life she has now, she describes her life as a miracle. "I am overwhelmed with God's good favor. I cry out to Him daily, asking Him how He can use me. I desperately want our lives to honor Him." She embraces the ever-present hand of God as she hems in her family when facing obstacles. She darns financial holes and often works against the grain of common economics and decisions. "We didn't qualify for a loan for our first home. It was only with the help of others that we became first-generation homeowners in our family. We dedicated our new house to God and even named it God's Dwelling Place. Today I work with people who'd never have believed they'd have a chance to own a home. God uses me daily, and I walk in God's authority. I am tenacious when others cannot see hope or believe in themselves. I fight for them when they cannot, and I encourage them to take their ground."

What authority has God bestowed on you for others? What would it look like in your life to grasp His authority with assurance? Living for the Lord is purposeful and always profitable for His kingdom.

May I pray for you? Strong woman, God made you in His image (Genesis 1:27). He blessed you with every spiritual blessing

(Ephesians 1:3) and gave you a spiritual gift to be used while serving (1 Corinthians 12:4). Extend your hand with confidence and authority. When you do, you represent the hand of God.

Yud's Song of Strength

A *distaff* is the holding staff for flax, or wool, from which the thread is drawn in spinning by hand. It also symbolizes the woman who holds it. What comes to mind when you think of a spinster? I imagine a lonely old woman. A spinster is defined simply as one who weaves and developed from the word distaff. Traditionally, women were the weavers, and their skill offered great honor and value. Weaving is referred to six times in this Proverbs 31 passage. One commentary notes, "Had this single praise been uttered of her, it would . . . be of itself a high commendation. [Rabbis] record an old saying of the Hebrews, that there is no wisdom in a woman but in the distaff; implying, as do the words of the text, that a woman's great praise is her industry."[3] Her work is important. "It is reasonable to conclude that being referred to as a distaff or a spinster would be a compliment, not an insult. But somehow we find ourselves far removed from the original intent of what God created to be beautiful and encouraging, into became something not quite as lovely."[4] Those who held a distaff and spindle in their hand were strong, well-skilled, and patient, and they demonstrated endurance as they completed this arduous task. She was a blessing.

I'm amazed when others relate stories to me of abundant blessing. Someone gave them a car or a check mysteriously arrives in an exact

3. Anne Pratt, "She Layeth Her Hands to the Spindle, and Her Hands Hold the Distaff," Anne Pratt: Proverbs 31 Verse 19 Commentary, *Blue Letter*, accessed October 29, 2019, https://www .blueletterbible.org/Comm/pratt_anne/EWPro31_19.cfm.

4. Sunny Shell, "Proverbs 31:19—She's a Distaff," *My Second Love* (blog), accessed October 29, 2019, https://www.mysecondlove.net/2008/09/proverbs-3119-shes-distaff.html#.XTipt -hKhPY.

amount. *Yud* is this open, extended hand of blessing, and Lisa is this type of person. "I firmly believe everything I have is God's. He tells me to give things away, so we've gifted several vehicles and any other resource He entrusts us with. It's not ours." When you walk in His freedom, you want everyone to experience it. She now mentors others in business and faith. "It's not that we talk about our faith. It's that we walk out our faith." She runs her family's real estate business with the same God-given authority with which she manages her home. "My husband is my coworker and my best friend. He is long-suffering. He has to be because I was so messed up when we began. But now, this messed-up little girl is raising mighty men of God. I want to help others as I was helped. My struggles help me understand the needs they face. I have experienced God's grace, and I can extend it to others."

The verse provides a reference to spinning, but today most women do not weave. Yet the Word of God must apply to modern woman. *Yud* holds a lesson for us through a metaphorical comparison to weaving. Titus 2:5 describes women as discreet, chaste, keepers at home, good, and obedient to their husbands. This is a verse I once read with my teeth tightly clenched. The phrase "keepers at home" is the Greek word οἰκουργούς, which consists of two separate words, *oikos* and *ergon*. *Oikos* means a household or family. *Ergon* is work or deed. It refers to the desire, intention, purpose, and noble action of the accomplished hand. The same word refers to the work of Jesus in Luke 24:19 and the works of God in John 9:3. Two valuable and revered women mentioned in the growth of the church, Lydia and Tabitha, were weavers. They wove into the fabric of the church and those around them, and they were honored. Strong woman, you can hold this honor. This is more than housework. This type of weaving holds, guards, and creates with the authority the workmanship of God's hand.

Pause and Reflect—Discussion Questions

1. Do you knit or crochet? Did your mother or grandmother teach
   you? Share your experiences.

   _____

   _____

   _____

   _____

   _____

2. What type of family manager are you? Do you lead and direct or do
   you micromanage?

   _____

   _____

   _____

   _____

   _____

3. How would you define authority? Do you have authority because of
   your position in a family or because of your responsibility?

   _____

   _____

   _____

   _____

4. Do you remember a specific time when God's hand held you? How has He empowered you?

_____

_____

_____

_____

_____

Praying the *Alef-Bet*

Lord, You give us great authority in life. As women, we so often weave into the lives of others. Lord, may I always recognize the responsibility I have to honor You in all I do. Thank You that Your outstretched hand is always available to me. Amen.

ב

She Extends Her Hand of Service

Kaf—the Cupped Hand, the Wing

PROVERBS 31:20

The imagery of a hand of authority was introduced with the last verse, and now, in Proverbs 31:20, the strong woman is extending her hand (*kaf*) to those in need. Since two Hebrew letters have the word picture of a hand, it is important to know their differences. *Yud* carries the idea of power, authority, and ownership through an open palm. *Kaf* is represented in the picture of a cupped hand including the wrist that holds, molds, and shapes anything that is put into it, into a form like itself. The shape of the letter helps us see the word picture of the cupped hand or a wing, but it also alludes to the ideas of productivity and accomplishment through the effort and work of the hands.

As we read the verse, we can imagine the strong woman cupping the hollow of her hand and extending it to the poor. As the memory trigger, *kaf,* her hand, is the focus in a telling picture of service and kindness. If we follow the development of the word *kaf,* we learn the word also includes a reference to bending or bowing down. With this additional meaning, we can add the imagery of the strong woman humbly bowing to others as she reaches out her hand in service to the poor.

She Extends Her Hand to the Poor, and She Stretches Out Her Hands to the Needy

The word for poor here is *aniy*, and it means depressed in mind and circumstances and to be humble. Most commentaries suggest this virtuous woman is serving the destitute in her community, which is a valuable, applicable lesson. But through added word study, we can see that a strong woman will also extend her hand to serve because of another critical need she recognizes: their poverty of spirit.

If you are poor in spirit you are still destitute and a beggar. You are crouched or bent over because you have not received the knowledge of God's eternal life or the riches of the kingdom of God. A strong woman recognizes this need in others, and by kneeling to extend her *kaf,* she offers help because at one time she too was bent over in her need.

As the child of an American diplomat, Kathi grew up in Lebanon. School, friendships, and caring for stray animals are some of the fond memories she recalls from living overseas. But memories of fear and danger also bubble up from her past. A man living in her family's apartment building abused Kathi for several years. Another shadow in her past is the memory of a man pretending to ask for directions while she walked in her neighborhood with a friend. The man abducted them in his car. The door handles and window mechanism had been removed. There was no way to escape. Through a series of misdirection, they found themselves in an alleyway that prevented the driver from pursuing them when the car door opened unexpectedly, and they bolted out. Years later, God revealed to Kathi through a prayer ministry session that His hand had opened the door for them and escorted them to safety.

During the height of the Arab-Israeli crisis in Lebanon, Kathi's family and other Americans were forced to flee their homes. Kathi remembers her mother leading her and her sister through frightening streets to an awaiting flight, which spirited them to safety in Europe. They were instructed to trust no one and tell no one. Their safety depended on it.

Her father stayed behind to secure documents and encourage other Americans to evacuate. For several days, their family was separated with no word from her father. At that young age, Kathi understood the pervasive nature of fear and the depth of her poverty.

Like Kathi, the poor in spirit are those in need of salvation. Matthew 5, commonly referred to as the Sermon on the Mount, is a picture of the journey to salvation. The poor in spirit recognize their sin and lack of a protective savior, and we mourn this knowledge. Yet God offers us salvation under His protective hand, and we receive Him. In accepting His hand of grace, we become meek. Some versions of the Bible translate the word as "humble," but both words hold the understanding of bowing as you would to honor someone. We do this in honor of our Savior Jesus Christ. Finally, as we grow in Christ, we will hunger and thirst for righteousness and will only be satisfied through Him. Do you recognize the poor in spirit in your life? How can you assist them in discovering the protective covering of God's wing?

Isaiah 61:1 presents the same message of sharing the gospel to the poor in spirit. Isaiah writes, "The Spirit of the Lord GOD is upon me, because the LORD has anointed me to bring good news to the afflicted [poor]; He has sent me to bind up the brokenhearted, to proclaim liberty to captives and freedom to prisoners." The words *afflicted* here in Isaiah and *poor* in Proverbs share the same root, *anah*. They hold the same understanding of becoming low, humble, and bowing down. Proverbs 31:20 shows a strong woman will extend her cupped hand and offer the Bread of Life and the thirst-quenching Living Water to all who are afflicted and poor in spirit. You can extend your hand to others in the same way. Being humble and meek is not the same as being walked on or weak. Humility is the recognition of an opportunity to honor the needs of another over yours and bow to them in honor.

There is no greater need than the salvation of Jesus Christ. Yet it would be several years before Kathi fully recognized the extent of her spiritual poverty. Until someone extended their hand to her need, she did not understand His care and His provision. She humbled herself before His throne to receive His reward of grace (James 4:6). Kathi began her relationship with Jesus when she returned to America through a simple prayer she said with her mother. But she was unaware what her life of faith entailed. "I loved God and His Word, but He was just there, a little distant. I knew good things were supposed to happen when I prayed. My embedded fear, though, prevented me from experiencing the Jesus who carries peace." Can you relate? Has fear ever prevented you from fully experiencing all Jesus has to offer?

As Kathi's faith grew, she began to discover the limitless depth of God's love and the power of the Holy Spirit. She encountered Jehovah Rapha, God who heals. "As He led me through my healing from fear, my depth of love grew. I began to better understand the extent He wants us to experience in our relationship with Him. God who heals, loves, and protects is not just our Savior but our Redeemer. My relationship moved from strictly obedience-based to a motivation derived from my love for Jesus. So many of us do not acknowledge the baggage we carry as we come to the Lord. Those experiences, beliefs, and traditions filter out much of how we can experience God in life."

This is an aspect of Kathi's story I can relate to. When we remove the anxiety that accompanies following a checklist of obedience, our lives begin to take on the image God desires. My own people-pleasing perfectionism prevented me from experiencing the fullness of God's pleasure. It's not that I wanted to vilify my sin or brush aside its consequence, but I let my failures define me for a time. Not only was I poor in spirit, I had a crippling case of "poor me."

I was convinced someone who grew up with meager financial means and with a history of making poor decisions, as I did, wouldn't be acceptable to God. I pursued degrees, careers, and programs to earn validation. But here is the rub: I exhausted myself working to validate my accomplishments—to myself. My life was filled with the feeling of not being good, smart, skinny, or cool enough. I allowed that insecurity to prevent me from entering any type of ministry.

God put women into my life at that time who extended their hand of friendship and confirmed God's love for me. My friend Debbie explored the Bible with me and challenged me to dig deeper. I experienced a joy in learning Greek, Hebrew, and history when I was previously convinced it would be too difficult. My friend Cyndi called me her kindred friend because I stuck with her through thick and thin. She didn't know me as the boring, shrinking violet I saw myself as. She knew me as her steadfast friend. Stacey, a friend I've known since junior high, refers to me now as her teacher—not the troublemaker who persuaded her to stay out past curfew when we were kids. It blows my mind.

Each of these women taught me in their own way to tuck myself under God's protective wing and submit to His leadership in response to my love for Him. His wing, His *kaf*, offers peace and refuge in the face of doubt and insecurity. He encloses me in the shadow of His wing (Psalm 17:8) when I feel vulnerable and exposed, and He supports me in His cupped hand when I grow weary from trying too hard to be someone I'm not. Even the ugly duckling had to seek protection as it matured into a beautiful swan, but when it did, it took flight. And so did I by fully embracing my identity in Christ. I was no longer poor in spirit but free indeed.

Kaf's Song of Strength

As we've seen, Proverbs 31:20 encourages us to assist the financially poor, but it includes the spiritually poor as well. The description of the strong woman stretching out her hand to others reveals her abundance of grace toward others (through *kaf*) and her protective power (through *yud*) as well. This reminds me of the role of a priest in God's kingdom. The Hebrew word for priest, *kohen* begins with the letter *kaf*. With its word picture, "a priest is someone who is molded according to what

God says."[1] Jesus has extended His hand to us, the poor in spirit. The appropriate response is to recognize our poverty before the hand of God. As He holds us in His cupped hand, we will be molded into His image so we can continue the cycle by offering others the opportunity to say yes to Christ. And guess what? The Hebrew word for yes is *ken*. And yes, it begins with *kaf*. Its word picture tells us that when we say yes we are opening our hand to life and activity.

Today, prayer leads Kathi's ministry with others. As a mentor, she prays with women who are struggling to overcome the effects of their pasts. Kathi's calling is to help them understand their image as children of God. Kathi adds, "Prayer is key as they work through forgiveness and understanding who they are in Christ. So many women believe they are marred for life. They need to forgive themselves before they can forgive others. They must move from a place of only knowledge of God to experiencing God's love and grace. Otherwise, how can you love your neighbor if you don't know how to love yourself?"

God often causes us to live out our purpose in the natural world before He will use us in the spiritual world. Kathi recognizes the needs of others because she has experienced that same need. "The care that first showed itself as a small child who tended to stray animals moved me to consider the physical and spiritual needs of the people God puts in my path today. This helps me understand and recognize the protective care Jesus provides me so I can extend it to others. Our identity in Christ can be experienced here on earth. It doesn't wait to be revealed when we get to heaven." Her philosophy, whether dealing with a financial, physical, or spiritual need, is to direct them to God for their sustenance. She introduces them to the God of healing, love, and redemption. She also reminds others, "We should never do ministry out of an undertow of weary obligation but out of overflow." That overflow comes from extending our hand to God first and receiving His abundance.

---

1. Hutchens, *Hebrew for the Goyim*, 91.

Kaf reminds us to be molded and used by Christ, our ministering priest. I pray you will understand your value as a godly woman, no matter your background or current situation. Whether you are single or married, have children or not, your bridegroom Jesus sings over you. Strong woman, I pray you will say yes to Christ, take His outstretched hand, and offer the same to others in need.

Pause and Reflect—Discussion Questions

1. Who has had an impact on your spiritual life and journey and how?

_____

_____

_____

_____

2. How do you serve others outside of your immediate family?

_____

_____

_____

_____

3. What part of Kathi's story do you relate to?

_____

_____

_____

_____

4. How did you recognize your poverty of spirit?

_____

_____

_____

_____

_____

5. What poverty in character do you recognize in yourself? How does God's Word help you to see yourself as God sees you?

_____

_____

_____

_____

_____

Praying the *Alef-Bet*

I'm going to use our prayer time a little different today and close by praying over you a paraphrase of another biblical song found in Psalm 45:1–4. Allow the song to wash over, strengthen, and encourage you. Strong woman, His heart overflows with a good theme, and His tongue is the pen of a ready writer. You are fairer than the sons of men, and grace is poured upon your lips. God has blessed you forever. Gird His sword as yours in splendor and majesty. Ride on victoriously for the cause of truth, humility, and righteousness. Let His right hand teach you awesome things.

ל

She Learns, Leads, and Guides

Lamed—the Teaching Goad

Proverbs 31:21

I must admit, I'm a bit of a nerd. As a schoolteacher, I enjoy doing research and learning, and I get a bit giddy when school supplies start arriving on store shelves. So I can relate to the next letter.

We might see a hint of our modern letter L in the ancient word picture of an oxgoad or shepherd staff. For the master, the oxgoad is the object of teaching used to prod, motivate, and redirect the oxen. There are some days I wish I could use a goad to prod my twelfth graders along.

Lamed stands in the center of the Hebrew alphabet as the tallest letter. Some Jewish commentaries suggest this stresses that our primary responsibility is learning and teaching God's Word. In Hebraic thinking, learning is insignificant and worthless unless our actions reflect the lesson. A lesson all believers can apply.

She Is Not Afraid of the Snow for Her Household

You may be asking how snow and clothing relate to leadership and teaching. The Proverbs woman takes significant steps in preparing her home. She embeds God's wisdom into her life and teaches her household everything she knows. She does not fear the metaphorical cold of a bleak winter, a season we all face at some point in life. If anything happens to her, they are well prepared.

Is studying and learning the Bible your thing? Or do you have a hard time understanding the Bible and how it applies to you today? At one of the first Bible studies I attended, I was amazed at the teacher's depth of knowledge. I remember thinking, "How in the world does she know all this?" When I sat down to read the Bible it did not hold my attention, and at times it was confusing. I wanted to understand like that teacher did. I asked God to give me a hunger for His Word, the ability to understand, and opportunity to study. His answer led me to Proverbs. Proverbs compares two women, Lady Wisdom and the Woman of Folly. According to Proverbs 22:15, folly is childishness, and the rod of discipline should be used to drive it far from her. This rod is an example of *lamed*.

I imagined the rods of Proverbs as implements of severe punishment. Something the ancients used to teach their children submission. You know, "Spare the rod, spoil the child," which, by the way, is not a Bible verse. The Bible does state, "He who withholds his rod hates his son, but he who loves him disciplines him diligently" (Proverbs 13:24). Rod, as used here, is the same word for rod, or scepter, used in Esther 5:2, *shebet*. Word studies describe this rod as a staff, a portion measured, instruction, and a scepter of a leader, chief or king. I can't find one example of Jesus beating someone into submission to become His follower and learn from Him. He did discipline through invitation and instruction. On a scale of one to ten, with one being not understanding and ten being a biblical scholar, how would you rate your level of biblical learning? What topics do you want to learn more about?

Linda is a twice-divorced woman who lives in isolation from the effects of a chronic illness. Can she possibly be a Proverbs 31 Woman to learn from? Oh, yes, she can. Linda grew up in the church and relished in the liturgical rituals of mass. She understood Christianity required a commitment to Christ and willingly made that commitment, to the point of wanting to become a nun. I'm glad she didn't because I might not have been born. Linda is my mom.

When I reminisce about my childhood, I don't particularly remember baking cookies with my mother or doing girly things like getting pedicures. What I do remember is my mom sitting in our living room in an overstuffed chair. The lamp standing on the floor next to her adjusted so she could read her Bible. If I needed her in the evening, she could be found in that chair pouring over the wisdom of God's Word.

Being smart is not the same as being wise. Wisdom comes from experience, a well we can all draw from. If we feel we are lacking in any way, Jesus promises to give us a spirit of wisdom (Ephesians 1:17). Ecclesiastes 12:11 tells us the words of the wise are like goads (lamed). God prods us along to continue learning, to obey a calling, and to critique our lives. When my students have questions in the classroom, I don't directly answer them. Instead, I might have another student help. You see, the best gauge I have in determining my students' learning is to see if they can teach. I'll listen and redirect if needed, but if a student can give an accurate explanation, they have learned. We can replicate this idea when sharing God's Word. Deuteronomy 6:6–7 tells us God's Word is to be on our heart and to teach it diligently. We are to share God's Word when we sit, walk, lie down, and when we rise. Knowing God's Word intimately provides an answer to everyone who asks for the reason why we have hope (1 Peter 3:15). How confident do you feel sharing God's Word?

I think of my mother as a biblically wise woman. She draws from familiar memories to teach me how God lead her through life. Mom struggled after she and my dad divorced. She said, "I was a Catholic, and getting a divorce meant leaving the church. The priest knew what was going on because I poured out my heart during confession, and he was very supportive. I feared the church wouldn't receive me the same."

During this time, Linda met a woman who became a lifelong friend. "My friend was a little older than me. She tucked my family under her wing and pointed me to the Lord. She loved me, parented me, and shared with me her simple faith. Her faith was not just a ritual but a personal relationship with Jesus. Her love for Jesus was expressed without the worry of deep theology. Her sweet comments were beautiful reminders that Jesus loved me, and that was all I needed."

Surviving the long winters in your life will only happen as you face the blinding snowstorms with an intimate knowledge of God. *Lamed* is His Word and Spirit directing you. How do you receive His leadings? Do you kick against the goads like Paul did in Acts 9:5, or can you accept the guidance of His loving hand and prepare for the next season?

For All Her Household Are Clothed with Scarlet

Scarlet was an expensive dye. This woman of Proverbs spared no expense to have her family well protected. However, the word *scarlet* can be translated as "double," which reinforces the idea of her complete preparation to endure the elements of winter. We will soon become cold and wet in the snow unless we wear multiple layers of clothing. Or if we have a second, or double, set of clothes, we can change and be dry and warm.

There is a spiritual application in this example. Her household is clothed in crimson or scarlet, the color of blood. The wording "makes it a natural symbol for purification and redemption."[1] The family is doubly clothed, or they put on the new. They are doubly born or born again. What better preparation is there for the winters of our life than being doubly covered by the scarlet blood of Christ? Modern readers who value the power of Jesus Christ can appreciate the wordplay in this verse. When you accept Jesus Christ and His teachings, God sees you as clean and as white as snow.

---

1. Dorothy Kelley Patterson and Rhonda Harrington Kelley, eds. *Women's Evangelical Commentary: Old Testament* (Nashville, TN: BH Publishing Group, 2011), 1046.

As the cold winds of winter crept into her life in the form of a chronic illness, Linda's second husband abandoned her. This dismal winter season has remained with her for nearly thirty years. The cold reality of living with a long-term, chronic illness forces her to face the unknown and years of loneliness. Linda's need for Christ's training and direction just to survive her disease is her momentum for growth in Christ.

"Because of my illness, I can't attend church, and the church rarely comes to me. I spend my time studying, praying, and crying out to God. Growing up, other than my one friend, I lacked examples of godly women. My training is through my mistakes, and the prod comes from God. I didn't know how to combine the isolation of my disability with being a mother or a grandmother. God had to teach me. The prodding hurts, but it is the winter of our soul that leads us down the correct path. You must trust the not knowing. That time of the unknown is the time of His staff prodding. You must seek the Holy Spirit and Scripture and give up your agenda, reasoning, and understanding. You don't move until you've surrendered to the prod." What lessons have you learned as a result of God's prodding? Can you identify times in your life His *lamed* has been a tool of redirection? Of discipline?

Lamed's—Song of Strength

In my experience, not every child is a willing learner. Much of the time they lack motivation and must be prodded along and encouraged to put into action the truths they learn. The Bible tells us, "Train up a child in the way he should go, even when he is old he will not depart from it" (Proverbs 22:6).

This verse has been interpreted several ways. It is often taught as a promise, that if a parent trains his child in the ways of the Lord, the child will not stray. Or, if he strays, he will eventually return. The verse may also challenge parents to recognize the child's unique personality traits and skills and train them to pursue their gifts. In any case, you can see that attention, time, and training is involved.

The phrase "train up" is only used three times in the Bible: Proverbs 22:6; Deuteronomy 20:5; and 1 Kings 8:63. In Deuteronomy and 1 Kings it is translated as "dedicated." The phrase "train up," *chanak,* indicates something initiated to the Lord for His use. Let's consider Proverbs 22:6 from this perspective.

> Dedicate to your child, speak over them, and the road they gather on when old, they will not turn off.

When we dedicate our children, or anyone under our influence, we are committing our time and the training we offer to the Lord for His use. We plant the seeds, but He produces the result. We initiate them toward a road, but only God knows their destination. We dedicate our children to Him, but only He can gather them if they turn off and away from Him. I say this because there are women who passionately follow Christ and invest well into their families, but they have watched the prodigals they love veer from the path to God they were faithfully initiated toward. Teach them to develop their own relationship with Jesus and pray for them. That is all God asks of you. It may seem impossible, but don't give up. The One who provides all wisdom and understanding can prod their return. Do you have a prodigal in your life? How does the new perspective of Psalm 22:6 encourage you?

Often the idea of teaching others is overwhelming, and we do not even know where to start. *Lamed* instructs us to have a heart for learning. In Hebrew, the word *heart* is spelled *lamed-bet.* The word picture emphasizes that the heart is the home of learning. You are yoked to the Holy Spirit of God. You have been blessed with every good and perfect gift (James 1:17). When you pray, "Teach me, oh Lord," a repeated phrase in Proverbs, God will respond. The strong woman makes progress toward this goal. Leading and teaching is never a one-time lesson; it takes continuous time. Here is the promise of *lamed*: if you teach and direct your family in the way of the Lord you do not need to fear the winters of life. Spring is coming.

Through Linda's surrender to God's plan in her life, she became a source of learning for others. "I was always praying for someone to study the Word with me. One day God clearly told me I had studied long enough. It was time for me to teach others." She became a Bible teacher for others who are homebound because of their illness. She teaches and leads through weekly Bible study conference calls and assists with the mentoring program at her church. She does not fear the winters of her life because she is surrendered to the leading of God and encourages others to better know Jesus.

"My illness separates me from everything. Others have a hard time accepting my restraints, and they often judge the requirements of my lifestyle. I understand how they feel because I tend to see the flaws before I see the divine. Judgment clouds my eyes. My relationship with Christ has shown me not to look to man but to Him. There is less pain in the learning when I turn to God quickly."

As a Proverbs 31 Woman, Linda represents *lamed*, God's implement of learning and teaching. Isolation, loneliness, chronic illness, or even a lack of knowledge does not have to limit our ability to teach and lead others. We can be used by God to prod others in the right direction with honesty, love, and the simplicity of our faith. Share with others the scarlet robes of salvation so they too will not fear the winters of their life.

Pause and Reflect—Discussion Questions

1. Share a fond memory you have of learning something from your mom, grandmother, or another woman of influence in your life.

_____

_____

_____

_____

2. What was one thing you wish you had learned growing up?

_____

_____

_____

3. Who are your spiritual mentors?

_____

_____

_____

4. What goal would you like to set when it comes to learning or teaching?

_____

_____

_____

_____

5. How much time do you spend reading God's Word? How often do you challenge yourself to memorize it?

_____

_____

_____

_____

Praying the *Alef-Bet*

Lord, give me a spirit for learning. Correct me if I have learned something in error. Redirect me if I am on the wrong path. Use Your Word to teach me and give me a heart and mind to read and understand Your Word. I ask for wisdom, Lord, as I teach those under my influence.

מ

She Is Washed Clean

Mem—Water, Life, Chaos

PROVERBS 31:22

Since ancient times, the word picture for *mem* has been linked to water. It carries the idea of chaos, like a raging ocean or turbulent water traveling downstream. *Mem* is a root letter in the words *mother*, *origin*, and *womb*, and is used as a prefix to indicate the female gender. The Hebrew word for mother is *em*, spelled *alef-mem*, אֵם. Its word picture represents the mother as "the strong water (like water that never fails, she is the lifegiver, around her grows an oasis of life)."[1] Can we just pause a second and celebrate that powerful word picture? *Mem's* link to life-giving water and women links it to the additional meanings of birth, life, and nations.

She Makes Covering for Herself

Proverbs 31:22 is the only verse in this passage that references the Proverbs woman caring for herself. One commentary notes she is "devoted to others but does not neglect herself. . . . She has a sense of her own dignity."[2] The

---

1. Franks T. Seekins, *Hebrew Word Pictures* (n.p., 2012), 62.
2. Fox, *Proverbs 10–31*, 896.

memory trigger is the word *marbad,* used to identify bed coverings made by this gifted weaver. Think of making your bed. You spread your sheets and a coverlet over your bed. Now relate *mem.* Just like a coverlet, water spreads and covers the land.

Psalm 139:13–15 describe our creation as being fearfully and wonderfully made. Our hidden frames were intricately woven in the depths of the earth. God's word holds the power of creation. He breathes over you and continues to cover you just as He did at the birth of the world. You are so worthy of His love and pride. You were made in His image. The God of the universe knit you together, wove all that you are, and spread you out on display with pride. Be proud of who you are and aware of the dignity God bestowed on you. Proverbs 31:22 is a reminder to take care of yourself and allow God to weave into your life so you can surrender into His covering.

Beth and Kathy are two women who have learned to lean in to the covering and dignity God provides. They learned to turn to Christ to calm the chaos raging in their thought life and cover their minds with peace. Mental illness and depression are not commonly discussed in Christian circles. Those struggling tend to mask their pain with a smile, avoidance, or the busyness of life. On the outside life flows on, but on the inside their emotions and internal conversations rush over them with a roar that drowns out any offerings of peace.

Beth is one who silently aches. As a child, Beth never felt as though she belonged. One side effect a child of divorce faces is dealing with the shuffle between families and schools. To make matters worse, Beth has alopecia and routinely losses her fiery red, naturally curly hair. A balding child isn't granted acceptance on the playground, and the rejection can be etched into a heart for life. She still loses patches of her hair today, and that old wound of self-worth reopens every time. This, combined with the diagnosis of a chemical imbalance followed by bipolar disorder, flooded her life at an early age.

Beth tells us, "I didn't know what the doctor was saying. I knew OCD behavior, rage, and depression, but I never linked that to bipolar. I thought bipolar was something like schizophrenia."

It was difficult for Beth to make friends, attend college, and hold jobs. Before she married, her life spiraled into drugs and drinking. She stayed in a neglectful marriage to an alcoholic for twenty-five years and yearned for her children to experience consistency, but it remained elusive. Like her missing patches of hair, a raw spot eroded into her heart as she faced a failed marriage and no idea how she was going to support her children.

What trials in life have you face that had you convinced you were going under? What thoughts flooded your mind as you walked through these times? How can you be strengthened through God's covering of peace?

Her Clothing Is Fine Linen and Purple

I'm hoping that references to fine linen and purple are prompting thoughts of the Tabernacle and the intricately woven tapestries displayed within. The strong woman's covering is clean white linen dyed purple and scarlet, just like the tapestries that covered the Tabernacle.

Exodus 28:4 holds another reference to wearing scarlet and purple linen. Exodus describes the garments of the high priest worn while serving the Lord and interceding for Israel. A strong woman serves in a similar position. In Proverbs 31:22, she is weaving a covering tapestry like those in the Tabernacle. She wears colors and material that represent the holy garments of the High Priest. And, like the breastplate worn by the High Priest, she wears her family and friends near and dear to her heart as she intercedes for them. She wears her priestly attire with dignity.

Beth struggled for years with the Christian life. In her mind, she experienced judgment, and the negativity raged. She never considered herself a part of the priesthood, but for years she studied the Word of God verse by verse and anchored herself to its truth. I asked how she draws strength from her relationship with Jesus Christ. There was a long pause and a deep breath before she answered. "I struggle so much. I battle my mind constantly, and the side effects of my medication are terrible. I've even considered suicide. When it gets bad, I just want to withdraw and hide. My life verse is Exodus 14:14, 'The LORD will fight for you while you keep silent.' I use Scripture and music over and over to make it through the minute, the hour, the day. Jehovah Jireh is my provider; He calms the storm."

What do you do to calm the storms raging in your mind? The healing waters of Christ can give life. When you assume your priestly position, you will be like a tree firmly planted by streams of water, which yields its fruit in its season, and its leaf does not wither (Psalm 1:3). As your roots sink deep into a relationship with Christ, you will long for Him more and more, and your soul will pant for Him just as the deer pants for water (Psalm 42:1). Until, ultimately, He will make you lie down as He leads you beside quiet waters (Psalm 23:2). What verse do you turn to in order to quiet your soul?

Mem's Song of Strength

I so often put the needs of others first and tend to neglect my needs. Do you do that too? The world tells us we must be fashionistas with flawless skin, be in perfect shape while holding down a job, and maintain an immaculate house while cooking Instagram-worthy meals. But providing for my family leaves me tired and with little time to take care of myself. It is more beneficial to measure myself against this Proverbs 31 Woman. She embodies the spiritual work-in-progress. Yes, that can be intimidating, but Christ is the first fulfillment of these verses. I don't have to obtain perfection; it is accomplished in Christ. When I look at the Proverbs 31 Woman, she is no longer a standard. Instead,

I recognize the value and strength I have through Jesus Christ. She becomes an example and a reminder to take care of myself spiritually and physically before I do anything more for others.

My sweet friend Kathy has walked through seasons of depression. In a four-year span, her mom suffered in a difficult death, leaving Kathy with the complicated task of handling her mother's estate. As a military wife, she and her husband were often apart. Her two oldest sons joined the military and were stationed on opposite sides of the world. Her daughter also married a military man and moved away. All this while recovering from major surgery after years of suffering in pain. She experienced wave after wave of crashing difficulties. She finally admitted her struggle.

"Admitting you are depressed as a Christian and as someone who everyone sees as a strong military wife is hard. People unknowingly can be so cruel. I have never understood depression. I've heard pastors say depression and anxiety is a sin! I don't think you can understand until you are there. I know in the past few years I have made mistakes because of my depression. I've asked for forgiveness, but I have been alienated and hated. Some have not granted me forgiveness, and that's okay. Even though it took me a while to get there, I know I am a child of the king! The only peace I experience is when I rely on the strength of Jesus. If I did not have Christ to lean on and depend on, I don't think I would still be on this earth."

In what felt like a baptism by fire, Kathy immerged with healing and experienced the soothing, living waters of God's peace and cleansing transformation. Have you ever wondered where the practice of baptism originated? Baptism stems from the Jewish practice of the *mikveh*. A *mikveh* is a collection of water, a bath, for ritual cleansing and purity. It offers hope. Three root letters in the word *mikveh—kaph, vav, and hei*—together spell hope. *Mem* added to the root word indicates a place from. The idea is that "hope and salvation comes from submerging our entire beings in the life force of G-d surrounding and filling us. . . .

The *mikvah* symbolizes death giving way to life, the place where hope is aroused and strengthened."[3]

How does this understanding of the tradition of *mikveh* help you understand the waters of baptism? Each is a symbolic representation of the washing away of sin and the birth of a new, transformed believer. How does this give you hope?

The *mikveh* represents purification for the Jew. Purity is the freedom from contamination. However, we will never be pure because we are born with the contamination of sin. Our words can be pure, our hearts can purely desire God, and we can dwell on the absolute truth of God's Word, but we are never pure before God without the cleansing and covering of Christ. According to Isaiah 58:11, His life-giving, satisfying water will never fail. Know that when we pass through the waters, He will be with us (Isaiah 43:2). We glorify Him by committing our hearts to Him. He completes the *mikveh*, cleansing and transformation within us.

Kathy and Beth are not alone. So many of us wrestle with anxiety and depression. I say *us* because even I have fought depression. Satan uses it to gain a foothold. Our struggle is not against flesh and blood but against the forces of darkness, the spiritual forces of wickedness in the heavenly places (Ephesians 6:12). When our minds are in chaos, we need the defensive weapon of God's Word and His peace that passes all understanding (Philippians 4:7).

Please hear me. Mental illness is not a struggle of our flesh. Mental illness is very real, and Satan uses its thundercloud of doubt to mount his attack. In counseling, those suffering the building storms of panic attacks are told to recite the Pledge of Allegiance or a something completely neutral in order to focus and calm the mind and stop the

---

3. Avraham Arieh Trugman, "Mikvah: The Art of Transition," Chabad.org, accessed June 17, 2019, www.chabad.org/theJewishWoman/article_cdo/aid/335957/jewish/Mikvah-The-Art -of-Transition.htm. If you are wondering why God's name was written as G-d, Jews believe in following Deuteronomy 12:1–4, God's name should never be written where it could be discarded or erased. And so, out of respect, His name is not fully written; the *o* is omitted.

destructive cycling thoughts. How much more powerful is the Word of God? It affirms for us the One who quiets the roaring seas and the tumult of the peoples (Psalm 65:7). When the waves rise, He stills them (Psalm 89:9). Jesus even holds power over the monsters that dwell in our overwhelming seas of chaos (Psalm 74:13).

Beth and Kathy know their only hope is to anchor themselves to Jesus. They are strong women, regardless of the hardships of their lives. They have slipped, and they have gone under; haven't we all? They continue to resurface. Christ's strength is like *mem*. His is our cleansing, transforming water. We must cry out for His peace against the choking surf of confusion. The anchor will hold. He is your strength and your very present help in time of need (Psalm 46:1). He loves you. Be washed, be anointed, and be His.

Pause and Reflect—Discussion Questions

1. Prayerfully consider how you can respond to God's calls to cleanse your life. What comes to mind?

_____

_____

_____

_____

2. Is there anything that prevents you from receiving God cleansing in your life?

_____

_____

_____

Praying the *Alef-Bet*

Lord, Thank You for the cleansing power of Your Word and sacrifice. Our minds can become a chaotic, raging river, but I pray Your peace washes over me and the fury of my storms. Lord, firmly plant me near Your streams of living water so I may live as the true daughter I am— the daughter of a King, clothed in royalty. Amen.

ן and נ

She Brings Honor
to Her Bridegroom

Nun—the Fish and Life

Proverbs 31:23

Like a character straight from the pages of Scripture, she found herself facing an unknown future. She once felt God's presence so deeply. But now, in the midst of tragedy, she could not hear His voice or feel His presence like she once did. Did He hear the cries of her heart? "I sought him but did not find him. . . . 'Have you seen him whom my soul loves?'" (Song of Solomon 3:1–3).

Nun is an old letter tracing back to ancient languages. All forms of the early word picture resembled a seed or tadpole. It eventually developed into the image of a fish. Pagan religions used the fish as a symbol of life and fertility, which is why the letter's imagery is linked to offspring, descendants, and action. *Nun* is a prefix indicating the future and holds the numeric value of fifty.

Nun is one of five letters known as *sofits* that are written either bent or straight depending on their placement in words. Jewish scholars equate the two forms of the *sofits* as ways we approach and serve God. One will approach God bent over in fear and reverence and another approaches standing straight, confident of God's love.

131

The Bible's first use of the word *nun* is in Exodus when Moses's right-hand man is described as "Joshua, the Son of *Nun*" (Exodus 33:11). Most commentaries will say *nun* is Joshua's father, but some indicate word-play. Joshua might be the son of *nun* because he was a disciple, a son, of Moses. Jewish sources compare Moses to a fish because Pharaoh's daughter pulled him from the water, which is what the name Moses means. Follow how Moses and Joshua personify *nun*. Moses (the fish, *nun*) led the Israelites out of Egypt to a new life (*nun*). Joshua, the son of *Nun* (posterity and future generations), followed in Moses's foot-steps and led them to a new life in the Promised Land to propagate and continue (*nun*). Isn't it interesting what a little Hebrew thinking adds to Scripture?

Her Husband Is Known in the Gates

Verse 23 is the central focus of the acrostic poem of Proverbs 31. Although it emphasizes the husband, it still reinforces the value of a strong woman. The Hebrew word for known, *yada*, is the memory trigger with *nun* used as a prefix for future tense. The husband will be known. To know, *yada,* suggests intimacy, to be so familiar with another you feel free to touch them. This does not necessarily refer to sexual intimacy but rather to personal. *Yada* indicates a willingness to share deep knowledge.

In the earliest of times, a city's life began at the gates and overflowed into the nearby market. The gates teemed with life and productivity. "The commercial, public, and judicial activities that took place in the gates were vital to the life of the community."[1] It was necessary for a man doing business at the gates to be known and respected.

A strong woman is a productive partner with her husband so he can focus on providing for and leading his family. She is his helpmate,

---

1. Fox, *Proverbs 10–31*, 896.

his *ezer*. An *Ezer* isn't a weak woman but a woman who backs her man with strength. Proverbs 31 praises the strength of this woman, yet the central idea is the husband and his honor in the community. "Her husband's prestige comes from his wife . . . It does not come from her beauty . . . but from her virtues and achievements, which the poem details."[2] He is known because he is in a partnership yoked together in love, from a home built on trust, through a beneficial relationship girded and protected in prayer available to him through the strength of his wife who is depending on Christ.

John MacArthur makes this observation of the verse, "He is esteemed and respected by his peers, in part because she created a world for him in which he could be everything God wanted him to be."[3] I pray this is my legacy. We work hard for our families so we can stand with pride and be known as honorable women. This is *ezer* in action. A valuable foundation for a married couple, as the poem implies. But what is the widow to do? The divorced woman? The single woman? To whom does she bring honor as an *ezer*?

Lauren grew up in a family who respected the value of church but lacked in-depth knowledge of Jesus. A curiosity of this unknown led Lauren to explore things further. Her family soon followed. Their experience at the trendy, contemporary church was vastly different from their traditional background, and soon questions began growing in Lauren's heart. "If all of this is true, what is keeping me from following Jesus? Why wouldn't I?" Lauren ached for this Jesus. She and her mom responded to the tug of the Holy Spirit together one evening. Her father's commitment to Christ followed six months later and her grandparents four years later. Her family encountered a radical transformation.

---

2. Ibid.
3. John MacArthur, *Divine Design: God's Contemporary Roles for Men and Women*, 2nd ed. (Colorado Springs, CO: David C. Cook, 2006), 84.

With a new life comes a new perspective. Lauren began pulling away from the popular and party scene. From a worldly standpoint, it appeared she lost friends and was alone, but her time was spent with the Lord, praying and reading her Bible. As she built her intimacy with Christ, she began to *yada*, know, Him. As she surrendered to His Spirit, He defeated any threat of loneliness.

How did you feel when you first became a believer? Some experience joy, others brokenness and sorrow. I felt a heavy need. The idea that God loved, forgave, and wanted to know me intimately was weighty as I realized how much I needed Him. He offered everything I lacked in life. Like Lauren, I too wanted to know this Jesus.

During college, Lauren pressed into Christ and learned the value of being still and quiet in His presence. She sensed God's prompting to change schools, an idea she describes as entirely random. To honor her growing relationship with the Lord, she fasted for confirmation, and His promptings led her to transfer from college in the sunny south to Chicago—in January. "My identity and everything comfortable were stripped and replaced with His deep intimacy."

What if we fasted from life to become more sensitive to God's voice? Lauren's story challenges me to question what areas I need to strip away to become more attuned to the Holy Spirit. How can God be honored if we do this? What depth of intimacy does He beckon us to but we miss because we are so busy?

Lauren's continuous surrender to the Holy Spirit placed her in the right place at the right time. She coincidently encountered a handsome young man over coffee who became her husband. She tells us, "The day we met, we talked all afternoon. Our time together seemed to slip away, but we made plans to see each other again, and again, and again. We met in October, he proposed in February, and we were married in June." He later told her that on the day they met he was praying for his future wife, and she was the gift of God's answer. Little did they know that their life would require God's *chayil*.

There is a difference between knowing about Jesus Christ and having an intimate *yada* relationship. Experiencing the depth of His love inspires praise. One of the Hebrew words for praise is *yud-ah*, very similar to *yada*. Both words contain the root letters YDH. The word pictures for these letters are *yud*, which means hand, *dalet*, the door, and *hei*, which represents breath or behold. When we praise, *yud-ah*, God, we behold His presence, and our breath is added to lifted hands. Praise occurs when we know God so intimately we can reach out and touch Him as we behold His presence. How do you experience God in your praise? It is my prayer for you to know, *yada*, God in such a way He inspires praise, *yud-ah*, in you.

He Sits Among the Elders of the Land

The Mishnah, a compilation of Jewish teaching, describes the Jew's life of sanctification. It was put to parchment well before the time of Jesus and established requirements Jewish men must meet at various stages of life. Schooling begins young. A man must marry before pursuing a career or assuming any authority. At twenty he can pursue his calling, at thirty he becomes an authority (this answers why Jesus waited until thirty to begin His ministry), and at fifty, he reaches the age of counsel. Don't miss that *nun*, as the central idea of this poem, represents the number fifty in a verse describing the husband sitting in counsel with the elders of the land. I pray my husband gains the influence of strong elders, like the men of Israel sitting at the city gates.

As Lauren's first anniversary approached, she and her husband joined Lauren's parents on vacation in Italy. Their desire to build a godly home often included quiet times, even on vacation. Although they normally did their own private quiet times, one morning her husband asked if he could join Lauren. Together, they read from Lauren's devotional. The devotion challenged that our greatest fear in life is death, but for a Christian, death ushers us into a new life. The day continued, and later Lauren asked her husband, "Are you excited to see Saint Mark's Cathedral today?" He lightheartedly responded, "I'm just excited to see Jesus today."

Their plans for the afternoon included a round of golf. As her husband teed off on the fifth hole, Lauren recognized he was not feeling well. As she brought him some water, her husband collapsed into her arms. He died tragically and unexpectedly in a foreign country, leaving her with unanswered questions churning through her heart. For days, weeks, and months she cried out to God asking why. She prayed as her husband died in her arms and felt the Lord's assurance that her husband would be okay. Lauren's perception of what that meant was different from the Lord's insight.

Have your circumstances skewed your discernment of God or your circumstances? It is so easy to slide our focus to our physical needs rather than an invisible God. As Lauren journeyed through grief, Jesus continued to woo her as the love of her life. He does the same for us. Nothing we face removes us from His hand. Instead, He holds us tighter and continues to whisper His love song over us. We need to quiet ourselves and listen. Realign our focus and allow Him to become our true bridegroom, as He did for Lauren. Our praise, *yud-ah*, cannot be based on our circumstances, our happiness, or the degree to which we feel blessed. We *yud-ah*, praise, Him because He is righteous and holy, yet He chose to know, *yada*, us. Lauren learned to honor Jesus despite her feelings and circumstances.

Nun's Song of Strength

For women divorced or not married, this verse may seem inconsequential. Married or not, as a follower of Christ, He is your Bridegroom. He is the One we make known at the city gates and the central idea of this poem. Proverbs 31:10–31 becomes the song your Bridegroom sings for you because of your praise and response to His love in your life. Just as the bridegroom rejoices over the bride, so your God will rejoice over you (Isaiah 62:5). Are you a bride who brings prestige and esteem to her Bridegroom, or do you foolishly tear Him down? Is your faith like a cold fish, or do you teem with life? Considering Christ as our groom changes our perspective of Him. I want my husband to be proud of me and value me. I want the same of Jesus.

It seemed Lauren had every reason to doubt God. "Just making it through each day, even walking to the mailbox, was hard. I faced the choking dryness of grief and contemplated turning away from Him." Grief came in waves, and everything reminded Lauren of her pain. She loved and grieved deeply. In her grief, she realized she desired the love of her husband more than the love of the Lord. This was acutely convicting. She clung to God's promise that He would not extinguish her smoldering wick of hope (Matthew 12:20). "I loved God so much. He loved me and revealed His extravagance, even during hardship. I knew I couldn't completely walk away."

Strong woman, do you believe, in the depths of your soul, that He desires to be your Bridegroom? Lauren did. "For me, He was like the bridegroom in Song of Solomon. I was walking through a season of His love I knew was my soul's dark night. My Bridegroom was drenched in myrrh, but I couldn't find Him (Song of Solomon 5:5–6). I was transitioning from 'My beloved is mine, and I am his' (Song of Solomon 2:16) to 'I am my beloved's' (Song of Solomon 6:3). The transition is from He's mine to I am His and, I had to ask, 'Do I still love Him when I don't feel Him, and He doesn't seem near?'"

Grief diminished as Lauren read Isaiah 6, which begins, "In the year of King Uzziah's death I saw the Lord sitting on a throne" (v. 1). As Lauren read, she substituted her husband's name, "In the year Art died you will see the Lord sitting on the throne." God's Word spurred a shift in her grief toward peace. "I desperately wanted God to show me how He was better than any other lover. He answered this cry of my heart through what I describe as a vision. I came away with my gaze locked on the Lord. He nurtured me to love like He does and to release my fear of loving again. I had to choose to love and be vulnerable with others even when it hurt."

The pain was freeing and worth it all. God lavished abundant grace upon her. Jesus again became her first love, her Bridegroom. "I felt free to love others again in a healthy way, enjoying them for however long they were in my life. No matter how painful the risk may be, God confirmed He would never leave me and could comfort me through any loss." So many of us miss this because we focus on our pain and not His presence. He is our Bridegroom. Anyone else is just a bonus.

Time passed, and Lauren met her second husband through her work in ministry. God's gracious gift of distance allowed their friendship to blossom through old-fashioned letters and email. However, she felt the timing was wrong and that somehow it betrayed her first husband. God did not mince words when He challenged her, asking, "Are you going to reject this gift because it doesn't meet your timing?"

Twelve years later, they have four kids and work in church planting. Lauren actively ministers to women and children through teaching and mentoring. She is beautifully gifted in intercessory prayer and discipleship. She walks gently with others in their grief from all forms of loss. This is not the ministry training she eagerly chooses, but it's used to honor her Bridegroom, Jesus Christ.

Honoring Christ is challenging when our dreams die or grow into the unexpected. Ponder for a moment how well the living God knows you, yet He will not forsake you. He has cleansed you with the waters of *mem,* and He gives you new life represented in *nun.* God so values you He inspired a poem at the closing of Proverbs in praise of your worth because your life, in all its form, brings Him honor and make His name known. Blessed is the woman who listens to wisdom and watches daily at the gates (Proverbs 8:34). Enter His gates with praise and thanksgiving (Psalm 100:4). Sing praise to the name of the Lord Most High (Psalm 7:17). Give thanks to His holy name (Psalm 30:4).

Pause and Reflect—Discussion Questions

1. What is God's image that you would like others to see in you? Do you present a façade, or do you offer an honest view that might include vulnerability? It might be beneficial to ask others how they perceive you.

_____

_____

_____

_____

_____

2. How do you live before others? How do you bring God glory? We aren't perfect. What areas in your relationship with Christ do you recognize as areas you should address?

_____

_____

_____

_____

_____

3. What gives you rest in Jesus Christ? How do you find peace in your busy life?

_____

_____

_____

_____

Praying the *Alef-Bet*

Jesus, You have washed me with Your cleansing waters of *mem*, and you offer me new life like *nun*. I am not perfect, and I am so thankful Your mercy is new every morning (Lamentations 3:22–23). Help me to live in such a way that I will boldly make Your name known and bring honor to Your kingdom. Surround me with elders I can depend on and learn from as though I were sitting with You at the city gates. I acknowledge I am worthy to be sung over, and I thank You for this gift in Proverbs to remind me of Your love for me. Amen.

ס

She Is a Valued Support

Samech—the Support, the Peg

Proverbs 31:24

A promise made in youth become a heavy burden to carry. How can Chris live with the consequences? "God, please hear the cries of my heart; change my husband's mind." Surely God wouldn't require her to keep a promised commitment made in the naïveté of youth. But what if He does?

The fifteenth letter of the Hebrew alphabet is *samech*, which is also a word meaning a prop or support. Some suggest the letter resembles a ring referencing infinity, with no beginning and no end. Combine the ring with the idea of support, and the imagery extends to a picture of marriage. In a Jewish wedding ceremony, the bride circles her husband seven times to signify her complete support for her husband. As a pledge of his unending support for her, he gives a wedding ring.

A goal in marriage is to work together, but when individuals have separate goals in life, this becomes a challenge. As a giddy teenager, Chris fell in love with her future husband after their first date. She knew he was *the one* and has never doubted it. But even while dating she knew their lives were on different paths. The man she loved did not want children. As a young bride she eagerly agreed. "I shared the same insecurities so many girls have. If the decision was no children, I was willing to agree with him because I didn't want to lose him." Have you done the same?

Are there times in your life you agreed to the disagreeable for the sake of peace or provision? Did it leave a bitter aftertaste, or can you now savor the decision? How does this apply to the Proverbs woman?

She Makes Linen Garments and Sells Them

Don't you love a good wedding? My children, nieces, and nephews, are all about the same age. They all finished college and became engaged like ducks in a row. Their engagements were filled with the plans of most engaged couples: booking vendors, finding the dress, and tasting menus. I might be a little biased, but their planning resulted in wonderful celebrations. But it is after the wedding that newlyweds embark on the never-ending journey of learning how to combine their lives and support one another.

As Chris built her life, she wanted to add a child. However, her husband did not waiver and stood firmly against having children. Chris earnestly prayed that God would soften her husband's heart and change his mind. "I never gave my husband an ultimatum or challenged him that if we didn't have kids, I would leave. I know other women in my position who have. Even though I was young when we married, I had agreed with him. As a Christian, I knew I made that commitment to both my husband and God."

One day, after a cross-country move away from family, Chris and her husband eagerly waited to close on a new home. With their worldly possessions sitting in a U-Haul, they wasted time browsing through a sporting goods store. Her husband, an avid bow hunter, stopped to admire a new bow. When he pulled the string back, pretending to sight his target, he lost his grip, and the cable guard penetrated his face just under his left eye. It severed his optic nerve and he lost vision in that eye.

Chris adds, "We closed on our house in a hospital room. Our new home had a nursery, and after the accident, I sat in that bedroom crying. I sobbed to my husband, 'What if I had lost you? I'd be alone with nothing of you.' His response was such a contrast from what I expected. He was thanking God we had never had children. He was worried that I'd be left alone to raise and support them."

Life continued, and friends had babies, frequently inviting Chris to their baby showers. "I got mad at God. I prayed for years to change Ray's heart, but God didn't answer that prayer." A divine appointment in a book she read sparked a change in her heart. "The introduction alone was convicting. I no longer prayed to change my husband's heart but to change mine. I needed peace from resenting a life I chose. It wasn't fair for me to keep pushing my husband."

What prayers have you realigned? How did they help you reach a turning point in your prayer life? God is only a teardrop away and desires to encircle you with His support.

Proverbs 31:24 presents a turning point in the acrostic poem. The new focus gives us a glimpse of the respect the strong woman earns from supporting her family. The memory trigger *cadiyn,* or linen, is a luxury item worn as an outer wrapping. She has handled linen, the fabric of priests, before, in verses 13, 21, and 22. How does a luxury item relate to *samech* and support? Perhaps it is more than just her industriousness.

In biblical times, couples didn't see each during their betrothal. Each prepared independently for their wedding and life together. When engaged, the bridegroom offered a gift to confirm his commitment to return to his beloved after preparations were complete. The bride was then responsible for making her wedding dress and being ready.

As believers in Jesus, we are living in the betrothal period between Jesus and His bride, the church. Jews also believe they are the bride of Christ. God calls Israel His betrothed in Hosea 2:19–20. Through the New Covenant and by grafting Gentiles into the rich root of Israel's olive tree (Romans 11:17), we are included as his bride. When Jesus ascended into heaven, He began our betrothal period. He promised to go and prepare a place for us, then to return and receive us (John 14:3). When our bridegroom, Jesus, returns to be reunited with us, we will be wearing clean white linen as our wedding attire (Revelation 19:8). We will wear this with pride because of the honor we bring to our bridegroom.

The lesson of *nun* encouraged us to make the name of our Bridegroom known. The idea that the woman of Proverbs is an allegorical representation of the church is nothing new. "So common has the equation of the Valiant Woman with the church become in the twelfth century, that preachers quote verses from it in their sermons to make a point about the life of the church . . . without bothering to explain the allegorical interpretation which makes this possible."[1] As the bride of Christ we must understand how to prepare ourselves while waiting for our Bridegroom.

> We are to love one another just as He loves us (John 13:34).
> We are to be devoted to one another, giving preference in honor (Romans 12:10).
> We are to be of the same mind toward one another, not haughty or wise in our own estimation (Romans 12:16).
> We are not to judge one another or put stumbling blocks in the paths of others (Romans 14:13).
> We are to pursue peace, be kind, and forgive one another just as Christ has forgiven us (Romans 14:19; Ephesians 4:32).

How do you honor your groom, Jesus? Some women find the task easy, while others feel unequipped or inexperienced. Before you begin to doubt your worthiness as His bride and instead listen to the arrows

---

1. Wolters, *The Song of the Valiant Woman*, 89.

of criticism and judgment the enemy shoots at you, I'd like to suggest you take advantage of a gift your Bridegroom has left for you while you await His return. It has a bit of a wordplay regarding the number sixty, the numeric value of *samach*.

Song of Solomon 3:7–8 describe a groom returning to see his beloved. He is traveling on a royal liter, surrounded by sixty mighty men. All of them are experts in war, and their right hands wield swords. Commentaries relate this passage to *samech*, and it serves as a reminder that God "surrounds us to protect us from the terrors of the dark."[2] This idea is supported in Psalm 91:4–5, which tells us God's faithfulness is a shield and bulwark. We do not need to fear the terror by night or the arrow that flies by day. As His bride you have committed to support Him. You are Christ's *eshet chayil*. His presence with us through the Holy Spirit is like the sixty men of Song of Solomon. He takes His position at your right hand to symbolize your protection.

What are your night terrors? Are they financial worry? A wayward family member? A job loss? Illness? Loneliness? Psalm 91:4 mentions God covering us with His pinion. The word is *sakak*, and *samech* is a root letter. *Sakak* means to cover, hedge, entwine, and wrap with protection. God promises to wrap Himself around us to keep away the night's terrors and enemy's arrows that hinder your heart's submission to Him. Struggling is a part of life, but worry does not add a single hour to our life (Luke 12:25). When the cycle of doubt begins, recall the lessons of Proverbs 31. As a believer in Christ, He gives you betrothal gifts. You are marked as His and worthy of the clean linen He provides. Entwine, wrap yourself with His promises, submit your heart to Him, claim His support, and know your Bridegroom celebrates you.

Chris had to shift her understanding of support. In God's lovingkindness and sovereignty, she never became pregnant. She has

---

2. Bentorah, *Hebrew Word Study*, 128.

never experienced the loss of miscarriage or faced the task of telling her husband she was pregnant with an unplanned child not fully desired.

"I still wanted to be a mom, but I had peace. It gave me the opportunity to love my husband through submission, supporting his wishes, and maintaining my commitment." She laughed, "Submission is hard. Women today hate that word, but it is a powerful way to honor and support both your husband and Christ."

And Supplies Belts to the Tradesmen

When women browsed the ancient markets, they interacted with merchants of the surrounding culture. By the Persian period, *Canaanite* became a synonym for *Phoenicians:* "great maritime traders who worked the entire Mediterranean basin."[3] As a result, the word *tradesmen* in this verse is a representation of the word *Canaanite*.

The Canaanites were Israel's enemy. When God gave the Promised Land to the Israelites, He instructed them to kill the inhabitants (Deuteronomy 7:1–2). Rather than obeying fully, the sons of Israel lived among their adversaries and their lives intertwined (Judges 3:5–6). To combat the enticement of the enemy merchants, the Proverbs woman was selective. She knew well the importance of keeping the commands of God's covenant. She was His possession among all the people and lived securely in the land (Exodus 19:5 and Leviticus 25:18). She knew practicing their customs would defile her (Leviticus 18:30).

From the beginning of time, God knew we too would live among enemies. Christ knew secular culture would be difficult to resist, so He prayed for our support (John 17:15). We do not know when the Father will say to our Groom, "Go, get Your bride," so we wait with expectation and continue to honor His covenant.

---

3. Fox, *Proverbs 10–31*, 896.

Chris knows her life without children does not resemble a typical woman's. As the only woman in her group of friends without a child, she realized a unique opportunity. Her calling to be childless is an opportunity to serve the women around her. "When you have children your whole focus in life changes. You barely have time for yourself, and serving anyone other than your family is hard. Some of the women around me were barely staying afloat, and I could serve and support them."

She leads weekly Bible studies in her home, hosts dinners, and uses her gift of service to create opportunities for women to have a few hours to themselves to fellowship with others and cultivate their relationships with Christ. As an aesthetician she encounters women who pin their worth on their outward appearance and do not understand their value as women created in the image of God. "We have an intimate atmosphere in the facial room. As they share their heart, I pray over them while I work. I can share that when I have the twinge of wanting a baby, or bitterness grows, or when I feel like an island in the sea of mothers and children, I can't take it out on my husband. My first reaction is to pray and reach out to Jesus for His support."

Chris relates to the story of Hannah. "I've learned the importance of prayer from Hannah and being real with God. Like Hannah, God answered my prayer and has made me a mother of many—not of kids but women." Chris reminds me of the woman represented in Proverbs 31:24. As a strong woman of God, and like the Old Testament priest, Chris lives a life of separation from the traditional pull of the world. It takes strength as a woman to agree not to have children. Perhaps it takes even greater strength to continuously honor the commitment and remain steadfast, even when we struggle to accept the impact of a long-ago decision.

What support do you need from God? Are you in a period of waiting and His answers seem elusive, or do you need to see through a decision? He desires to support those who are His (2 Chronicles 16:9).

Samech's Song of Strength

Everyone needs God's support and sustaining strength. Through her dependence on Christ, Chris became a *samech* of supportive strength for others. She weaves into her husband the support of honor, submission, and love. She weaves into others the support of friendship, encouragement, and the wisdom of God's Word. Her support is consecrated for the Lord.

The word *samech* is used in Deuteronomy 34:9, "Now Joshua the son of Nun was filled with the spirit of wisdom, for Moses had laid his hands on him; and the sons of Israel listened to him and did as the LORD had commanded Moses." Do you recognize any resemblance to support? In Deuteronomy, *samech* is rendered as laid hands. Moses placed his hands on Joshua and prayed over him a prayer of consecration and support. "To lay hands on someone is to involve a spiritual anointing or support for that person," like the priests placing their hands on a sin offering.[4] The priests did so to devote their offering before God and gain His support (Leviticus 3:2 and 8:14).

Christ, as our Bridegroom, has pledged His support to us as His bride. Our prayers call for His support spiritually in the natural world. The Bible records His response.

> When we seek Him, He will let us find Him (1 Chronicles 28:9).
> He doesn't forsake those who seek Him (Psalm 9:10).
> Those who seek Him find Him. He opens the door for those who knock. (Matthew 7:8).

The lesson of *samech* is to support what is weak, like a woman selectively navigating the enemy's market. Some days you need the support, other days you are the support. Your Bridegroom seeks you. You are more valuable to Him than jewels. He is seated at the right hand of God

---

4. Bentorah, *Hebrew Word Study*, 125.

and consecrates our prayers before His throne. Like Aaron and Cur, who lifted the arms of Moses when he grew weary from battle, Christ supports us.

Pause and Reflect—Discussion Questions

1. How do you feel about laying your hands on others in prayer?

_____

_____

_____

_____

_____

2. What does being a member of the entire bride of Christ mean to you?

_____

_____

_____

_____

3. How do you feel about the character and integrity of the bride (the universal church) today?

_____

_____

_____

_____

4. Married or single, what does Christ as your Bridegroom mean to you?

_____

_____

_____

_____

_____

5. How can His description of Bridegroom give you hope?

_____

_____

_____

_____

6. How do you act as a support for others?

_____

_____

_____

_____

7. What support do you feel you need from others? From God?

_____

_____

_____

_____

Praying the *Alef-Bet*

Oh, Darling of Heaven, I eagerly await Your return. Some days are hard, and I long for Your supportive, loving hand to lead me. As Your bride, I prepare for Your return by supporting the entire bride of Christ. I pray that while we await Your arrival, we will not lose the excitement and anticipation a bride has while she waits for the wedding ceremony. My prayers lift before Your throne knowing You intercede for me. Thank You for encircling me with Your never-ending love and support. Amen.

ע

She Looks to the Future
with Peace

Ayin—the Eye, the Source

PROVERBS 31:25

S tephanie is part of the 5 percent of children born as a result of rape. She was conceived under violent circumstances. Adopted at four days old, she grew up in a home with loving parents. What her parents did not know was that for ten years Stephanie was sexually molested at the hands her family members. Her abuse left a scar. "It really influenced how I saw relationships. By sixteen, I was the girl looking for love in all the wrong places with a very distorted view of true love. At seventeen I was pregnant, and by nineteen I was a divorced single mother. By twenty-two, I divorced again." It is easy to let our life's mistakes define us. Stephanie felt confirmed as worthless, a failure, even promiscuous, but she had yet to experience how God saw her when He looked on her with eyes of love and redemption.

Ayin's word picture is an eye, and it symbolizes understanding, perception, and obedience. Scholars suggest the written form of *ayin* shows two eyes that "represent choice or the action of the will . . . We can choose whether to use the good eye or the evil eye to perceive things."[1] If you look at the letter, the right eye is turned, looking at the left side where our heart is located. "This shows that our eyes, our insight, and consciousness will influence our heart."[2] Eyes have long represented sight and understanding. I'm reminded of some common idioms of today, such as, "The eyes are the window to the soul," which means to truly know someone we must look into their eyes. Or to say, "I see," means, "I understand."

Stephanie struggled with her self-worth, but what is your perception of how God views you? When God investigates your heart, what does He see? Can you celebrate when you look back and see how He has transformed you, or do you perceive areas still in need of God's insight? Viewing your life through God's eyes can give a refreshing perspective.

Stephanie describes her life before Christ as a train wreck. When she encountered Jesus, it was the first time she ever felt whole, pure, and loved. "Realizing I was not a throwaway girl was such a foreign feeling; I was valuable to Jesus." While living in government-subsidized housing, a neighbor shared with her the truth of salvation. "I knew of Jesus, but this woman explained salvation. I began attending church with her, and the Jesus I learned about was unlike any version of God I had heard before. I wanted salvation, but I was still hanging on to the lifestyle I was most familiar with. In my mind, I was saved, but my life hadn't changed." God strategically placed Scripture in her line of sight. Biblical pamphlets were left where she worked. A state trooper who worked with her also left her notes with Scripture.

The Bible tells us that faith comes from hearing, but for Stephanie her faith was built on tangibly seeing the Word of God. She finally came to a point where she no longer wanted to hold back. She completely

1. John J. Parson, "The Letter Ayin," Hebrew 4 Christians, accessed June 18, 2019, https://hebrew4christians.com/Grammar/Unit_One/Aleph-Bet/Ayin/ayin.html.

2. Matityahu Galzerson, quoted in *Learning God's Love Language: A Guide to Personal Hebrew Word Study* by Chaim Bentorah (True Potential: Travlers Rest, SC: 2018), 91.

surrendered every aspect of her life to God. She needed to experience the blessings of Proverbs 31:25 and smile at her future.

God sees you at your best and your worst, yet His love endures forever. You are the apple of His eye (Psalm 17:8). How have you drawn from His never-ending well of strength and insight like Stephanie? Are you at a place in your walk with Christ where you can smile at your future? If not, what would it take?

Strength and Dignity Are Her Clothing

I love this verse! If I could embody the Proverbs 31 Woman without hindrance, this is how I want to be seen: strong, dignified, and unafraid. These are the qualities Christ sees in us, and this poem is our reminder. The next six verses, 25–30, speak blessings over the Proverbs 31 Woman because of her firm foundation. You can do this! You can be this woman. Not perfect, not without doubt, but one day at a time through the strength, wisdom, and support of Christ. "The Woman of Strength wears fine attire as befits her status, but her true beauty comes from her spiritual strengths, manifest to all like elegant raiment."[3] God doesn't see us as man does. The Lord looks at the heart (1 Samuel 16:7).

Stephanie met her third husband in a bar. He was the drummer in a rock band who fully embraced the rock-n-roll lifestyle. She surrendered her life to Jesus after they married, and she risked him leaving. Her husband was the first to see Christ transforming Stephanie into a new creation. She was no longer an insecure, angry woman. She slowly began to understand the depths of God's love for her and knew her husband would not readily accept her needed change. She had no foundation to build her new faith on other than her hunger for Christ. She wanted to represent Christ well, so she became bold.

---

3. Fox, *Proverbs 10–31*, 897.

The memory trigger for Proverbs 31:25 is strength, *oz*. If you recall from *zayin* in verse 16, *oz* means mighty, force, strength, and fortress—another nod to the poem's military theme. Used here, it represents "a material force, a physical demonstration, and that which is vigorous, powerful, even audacious."[4] Audacious means bold and willing to take risks. I don't know about you, but I'm okay being described as audacious.

Oz is a word customarily reserved to describe Yaweh, as in the following:

> Psalm 28:7: The LORD is my strength and my shield.
> Psalm 93:1: The LORD . . . is clothed with majesty . . . and girded
>   Himself with strength.
> Psalm 118:14: The LORD is my strength and song.

It isn't a coincidence the Bible uses *oz* to describe the strength of a woman too. As we commit ourselves to Jesus, we begin to reflect the God we serve. By the way, did you notice in Psalm 93:1 that the Lord is "clothed in strength"? This expression is used biblically several times as a reference to military strength. God inspired the writer to honor your strength by referencing it four times in this Proverbs passage. How do others acknowledge God's strength in you? Do they mention your willing spirit, your determination, or the shoulder of support you offer others? You are strong, but do you consider yourself bold and audacious? You are. God says so.

God rewarded Stephanie's audacious behavior. Six months after her salvation, her rock-n-roll husband was saved. But the intermittent time was hard. "Light and darkness do not mix. He would provoke me, I'd lose it, and he would mock my response. Everything was new to me, and I tried to live what I was learning. He wanted his wife back, but she no

---

4. Hutchens, *Hebrew for the Goyim*, 117.

longer existed. I was transforming before his eyes, and I left Scripture for him to see everywhere. God was faithful."

Like the Proverbs woman, Stephanie clothed herself with dignity. Most versions translate the Hebrew word *hadar* as "dignity" or "honor," but it can also mean magnificence, an ornament, splendor, beauty, excellency, glorious, honor, and majesty. Dignity is nice, but can you imagine being described as glorious and with majesty? Oh, what a difference! *Dignity* is another word translated to fit the ideal woman of the fifteenth century. The words *majestic*, *splendor*, and *glorious* were saved for the king or for God. As you spend time with God, you reflect His majesty.

Moses spent time with God face-to-face. When he came away, God's reflection on Moses's face was so powerful it had to be covered (Exodus 34:29–33), even as it began to fade (2 Corinthians 3:13). Despite our circumstances, our past, or our struggles, we can still reflect His glory. We are the bride of a magnificent King. Christ dwells in us, and He desires for His glory to be displayed. The veil has been removed. If you struggle to accept this, may I pray over you?

Father God, remind us daily we are precious in Your sight. You bestow on us the gifts of magnificence, dignity, and strength so we can hold our heads high and boldly reflect You. I pray we are reminded that You are so much more than our circumstances, doubts, and struggles. You are the God of splendor and glory, and Your eye is on the ones you love. Remind us the hindering veils have been lifted, and we can shine because of Your gift, Jesus Christ.

And She Smiles at the Future

Can you confidently look toward the future and smile? For some, the future holds hope and excitement. For others, who can barely face a day, thinking of the future may be crippling. The woman of Proverbs looks to the future and smiles. The Hebrew word for smiles in this verse is *sachaq*, and it means to laugh, rejoice, to play. Oh, to have her confidence.

As Stephanie's faith developed, she realized the difference between condemnation and the Holy Spirit's conviction. At first, it was confusing. She didn't understand the wrestling in her heart wasn't a hot flash. It was the battle of her flesh. She also developed an insatiable appetite for God's Word. "People would discuss topics common in Christianity, and without an upbringing in the church, I was completely unfamiliar with each. I had to dig out doctrine and theology on my own. I had to learn how to study God's Word."

Stephanie's identity in Christ gave her peace as God revealed His plan for her life. She and her husband became missionaries in Costa Rica. The prospect of going was exciting, but the leaving was hard. Their confidence in Christ erased their fear and doubt. "We didn't get all of the work right. We were even robbed once, but we connected with the area's pastors and their wives, forming a supportive network. The idea of God allowing us to be a part of His works brings joy." Do you celebrate your calling? Does looking back at your partnership with Christ bring you joy, or are you still wrestling with God?

Ayin's Song of Strength

Proverbs 3:5 says to trust in the Lord with all our heart and warns us not to lean on our own understanding. Proverbs 3:7 warns us not be wise in our own eyes. Another warning is in Isaiah 5:20–21, which tells us, "Woe to those who are wise in their own eyes." *Woe* is really bad stuff. God has given us the ability to think and the freedom of choice. If you are second-guessing your understanding of a situation, He will never offer the soothing enticement of sin. If your marriage is failing, no matter how bad it looks, God does not provide a new man as the answer. If someone hurts you, keeping score or blasting them on social media is not a choice God offers. When you became a believer in Christ, you became a new creation with the ability to filter your life through how God sees you. When we revert to our old ways, bad choices will be made. Delight in Him, and guard against doing evil in God's sight.

The only reason the woman of Proverbs 31 can laugh at the future is because she made a choice to follow God. She is confident in her identity in Christ. If you truly want to laugh at the days to come, you must continuously look to God. Vision reveals more to us than any of the other senses. "It only takes one nerve fiber to carry sound to the brain . . . Yet there are more than half a million nerve fibers by which the optic nerve carries visual pictures to the brain! But for all its intricacy, the eye alone does not guarantee that a person will have correct perception."[5] Eyes need light to see clearly, and "the light of God is not meant to blind us to our sin but to reveal it."[6] A strong woman guards her heart against spiritual blindness.

There is nothing funny about a rebellious child, the hard places of life, knowing the cancer is terminal, or being defined by our past. Laughter comes when we know God is sovereign and we have eternal life in His glorious presence. Our laughter comes from our confidence in God's redemptive power, our transformation and reflection of His majesty. Our paths in life change quickly. In the blink of an eye, we can travel from a mountaintop to the lowest valley. But no matter our circumstances we can face tomorrow because of Christ. Do you believe this? We don't need to worry about tomorrow. It will care for itself (Matthew 6:34). I heard a wise saying once, "Worry does not help tomorrow, and it robs us of today's joy." I know this is hard to apply, it is but so worth it. Strong woman, smile, laugh, sing, and play. You are already made new.

---

5. Mills and Michael, *Messiah and His Hebrew Alphabet*, 90.
6. Bentorah, Hebrew Word Study, 133.

Pause and Reflect—Discussion Questions

1. Matthew 7:1–5 warns you to notice the log in your own eye before looking at the speck in your brother's eye. How do you respond when God allows you to see areas of sin in your life? How do you respond when you see sin in others?

   _____

   _____

   _____

   _____

2. What changes do you need to make in your life that will allow you to look more confidently at God's future for you?

   _____

   _____

   _____

   _____

3. What strength do others acknowledge in you?

   _____

   _____

   _____

   _____

Praying the *Alef-Bet*

Lord, Knowing Your eye is always on me gives me confidence to look toward the future. Knowing You are sovereign allows me to do so with a smile. I pray that You would enlighten any areas of spiritual blindness so that I might see Your truth clearly. Amen.

ף or פ

She Speaks with Wisdom and Kindness

Peh—the Mouth

PROVERBS 31:26

This earth was created as God leaned in and placed His face over the chaotic void. The Holy Spirit breathed forth from His mouth, and His creative power took the form of His Word. His breath continues through time, moving across the face of this earth. As long as we hold His breath in our lungs, His creative power is still at work in us and through us. He is the author of our faith, and our story is not complete. Our words hold power too. A simple sentence can destroy, leaving piles of rubble. But when we open our mouths and speak with wisdom and kindness, we can build with empowering words.

Looking at the pictograph of *peh,* some think the letter resembles a face. *Peh* is the Hebrew word for mouth, which lends to the letter's extended meaning of speech. *Peh* is another letter written in two forms—open and closed. The Talmud suggests this symbolizes the two positions of our mouth—open and closed.

The Hebrew word for face is *penay,* spelled with the letters *peh, nun, yod.* The accompanying word pictures reveal that the action of the mouth is in the hand of God or manifested through God's hand.

161

Oh, to truly submit the actions of my mouth and face to God's hand! Controlling my mouth can be hard at times. I'm afraid my mouth sometimes reveals the ugliness of my heart. Not that I'm particularly unkind, but my experiences and emotions influence what comes from my mouth, and it does not always reflect the beauty of God's grace, mercy, and loving-kindness.

As a high school teacher, I hear the shocking and ridiculous daily. God grants me myriad opportunities to practice this type of submission. I'm reminded of the social media meme that says, "Controlling my tongue is no problem; it's my face that needs deliverance." Can you relate?

The word face, *penay,* is also used in Exodus 20:3, which declares that we will have no other gods before Him. It can also be translated, "You will have no other gods *in my face.*" This verse states two important lessons for our relationship with God. First, we can't serve other gods, and, second, "God is saying, 'Don't let the words of any other gods (words from their face) take precedence over my words.'"[1] *Peh* shows us just how personal God is. We stand before Him face to face. Close enough to feel His mouth breathing life into us and over us. In response, may the words of our mouth be acceptable to Him (Psalm 19:14).

How successful are you when it comes to controlling your words? I continue to surrender the battle to Jesus as a work in progress. Biblically, the mouth gets a bad rap. It is boastful, full of curses, lies, deceit, and slander. One author noted, "Six millennia of sin have so eroded, warped, and polluted human language and speech that communication is only a shadow of what it should be."[2] If this is true, I respect the value of the closed *peh.*

There is hope. Wisdom and kindness from our mouths can be like a bubbling brook (Proverbs 18:4). The mouth of the righteous is as choice

---

1. Hutchens, *Hebrew for the Goyim,* 122.
2. Mills and Michael, *Messiah and His Hebrew Alphabet,* 98.

silver and will feed many (Proverbs 10:20–21). I'm hard pressed to think of anything more refreshing, especially when facing our darkest times.

She Opens Her Mouth in Wisdom

Cynthia grew up in what she describes as a strict Christian home. Her single mom valued the biblical foundations and support the church offered her family. Cynthia knew and accepted early that Jesus loved her, but she describes her early relationship with Christ as mundane.

When she met her first husband, she was thrilled to attract the attention of an older, worldly man. After eleven years of marriage, he met someone else, and her dreams of happily ever after were replaced with a living nightmare. "One afternoon he picked up the kids, and his girlfriend, who eventually became his new wife, was with him. I waved goodbye as my entire life drove off. She happily sat next to the man I loved, with my children snugged into their seats, all tucked in. As they left my neighbor joined me in the driveway and acknowledged how hard that whole scene was for me. He invited me to his apartment, and I followed." That day Cynthia's hopelessness thrust her into the nightmare of drug abuse. "I went from being the suburban soccer mom to eventually becoming the woman looking to score at a meth house. I was a mess. Despite losing teeth, wearing a sunken face, suffering in relationships, and the risk of losing my incredible kids, I only wanted to numb the pain."

To speak wisdom, a strong woman draws from her relationship with Christ, to whom she is yoked. *Peh,* or mouth, is the memorization trigger in this verse. It tells us a strong woman opens her mouth with wisdom. So it must be possible to speak with wisdom and to wisely know when to cry out for God's help. Have no doubt, Cynthia knew Jesus, but she slowly declined the strength His yoke provided. "Meth was my escape. The drug numbed my heart and my mind. I didn't have to respond or sometimes even acknowledge my feelings. I chose not to seek Christ. Instead of running to Him, I ran to drugs and unhealthy relationships."

What numbs your pain when you're at your weakest? Is it alcohol? Shopping? Hours at the gym? We all have something we turn to rather than seeking the face of God. Cynthia felt the biting shackles her choices had locked her into.

Chokmah, חָכְמָה, is the Hebrew word for wisdom. It is acute judgment, or a corrective lesson. When we apply God's wisdom, we make wise choices, and we can correct our wrong decisions. I like this definition. It tells me wisdom is a process, and I get do-overs when I fail. *Chokmah* is the same word in Proverbs 1:8 that Solomon used to begin Proverbs. It is used again here in Proverbs 31 as a bookend in the final chapter to reiterate this journey of wisdom. A woman of strength is hard to find (Proverbs 31:10). However, Lady Wisdom is available to all who seek her (Proverbs 8:1–3, 17, 35).

The Bible offers a parallel between the Proverbs 31 Woman and wisdom. Let's compare:

> An excellent wife, who can find? For her worth is far above jewels [*paniyn*]. —Proverbs 31:10

> Wisdom is better than jewels [*paniyn*]; and all things desirable cannot compare with her. —Proverbs 8:11

> The acquisition of wisdom is above that of pearls [*paniyn*]. —Job 28:18

Wisdom and a woman of strength are the only two items the Bible states as being more valuable than jewels or pearls (*paniyn*). Can you imagine the significance a strong woman of wisdom is to her husband, her family, and those in her circle of influence? The Bible calls her invaluable. This poem isn't a standard; it is a blueprint of priceless strength. When we yoke ourselves to Christ, allow Him to make His home in our heart, and navigate the process of learning God's wisdom—that is what makes us more valuable than jewels.

Blogger Craig Denison offers this insight. "The power of Scripture lies in the fact that its pages are filled with the words of a God who is still active, powerful, and loving. I went years using Scripture incorrectly. I viewed it as a set of rules I needed to read and try to keep rather than as a guide to experiencing the adventure of communion with my heavenly Father. I viewed Scripture as a chore rather than the words of God meant specifically for me. . . . My problem was that I hadn't experienced a life lived 'by every word that comes from the mouth of God.'"[3]

How do you view God's Word? In our darkest moments the wisdom gained from Scripture can pierce our hearts and respond with power. Even when we feel our worth is diminished. Cynthia agrees. "I remember one prayer. I told God I was not interested in praying for myself, I did not care how He responded to me, but I prayed for my kids. I asked Him to love them and keep them close to Him all the days of their lives."

Aware of her desperations, her family constantly ushered Cynthia's need into God's throne room through prayer. "I was betrayed, abandoned, and too angry to pray. The wisdom of my mother and grandmother's prayers was relentless. I was living against everything I knew that was right and good. After almost three years of drugs, which included times I considered my kids would be better off without me, I finally hit bottom.

One weekend, while my kids were with their dad, I finally accepted that drugs could no longer be an option. I called my mom and admitted my drug addiction. She already knew, and she immediately came to help me. She sat and cried with me as I detoxed, cold turkey. For

---

3. Craig Denison, "Man Shall Not Live by Bread Alone" *First15* (blog) July 3, 2016. https://www.first15.org/07/03/seeking-god-through-scripture/.

the next four days I was psychotic, I raged, vomited, and even soiled myself. Then my mom gathered me up and took me to her house where I slept for another three days. I was determined to get clean before my kids returned."

What truths of God's Word have you experience? Cynthia leaned into God and His promise that He would never leave or forsake her (Hebrews 13:5). She wisely responded to His truth. "Once clean, I changed everything in my life. I moved to a new city. The kids changed schools, and I have never used drugs again." Clarity confirmed God's provision even while slogging through sin. "In the despair of my drug-fogged brain, I recognized His constant presence. He even honored my prayer of protection over my children. God spared them from facing the dark consequences of my sin. I was in the absolute pit, but He was faithful. He heard me when I did not deserve it."

Cynthia's season of rebellion was grotesque, but God's grace was greater. She looks back on those three lost years and states with absolute certainty that God's faithfulness prepared her for the fight she faces today. She learned to live by God's every word. Little did she know she would once again stand face to face with God and call upon His strength as He breathed His life-sustaining grace over her.

And the Teaching of Kindness Is on Her Tongue

Kindness in Proverbs 31:26 is *chesed*, which describes how or what the woman speaks. It can also mean mercy and loveliness, which is *yapheh*, spelled *yud, peh, hei*. This word picture tells us "beauty is revealed in the deed spoken."[4] God's *chesed* is the loveliness of His mercy and loving-kindness.

A few years later, Cynthia met her second husband. He was strong and gregarious. God used him to redeem the lost years. A friend

---

4. Seekins, *Hebrew Word Pictures*, 78.

connected them, but before meeting they became acquainted through quick-witted banter on Facebook. He admitted that her four kids intimidated him, but he liked her sass, and his interest was piqued. The day they finally met, they exchanged more than two hundred text messages. "We met in early December. On Christmas, he came bearing gifts so personal and perfect for each individual child. I knew he had paid attention to our conversations and the details of my life."

They were engaged in June and married in March the following year. He knew Cynthia was broken with a heart shattered in the area of trust. "Rather than thinking me defective, he did everything he could to make his life transparent and build trust. Other than my Father in heaven, I have never experienced such redeeming love." His love overflowed and poured into her children. He included Cynthia's daughter, bringing her flowers and wooing her heart with gentleness and beauty. He coached her sons, attending every sport and school event. He missed nothing. He loved Jesus and his family *big*.

Cynthia's husband rarely drank to excess. He had a bad experience one time, which caused him to lose control and act out in anger. He never harmed anyone, but he was heartbroken that his angry words cut deeply those he loved. On a pleasant spring day, the day before Mother's Day, Cynthia's family hosted a chili cook off to fund an upcoming mission trip. "Our friends joined us, we raised money for a worthy cause, tasted chili, sipped wine, and danced on our patio. About midnight, during a conversation around the fire pit, it was like a switch flipped. He began making comments completely out of his nature. I even questioned if he was feeling okay." Her husband became enraged, stormed through the house, and left in a fury.

A few hours later, just before four o'clock on the morning of Mother's Day, the police knocked on Cynthia's door. They found her husband. As Cynthia listened to their words, she screamed for God's *chesed*. A bizarre chemical imbalance prompted by the smallest amount of alcohol had enticed him to take his life. "In that moment I vividly heard the Holy Spirit saying to me that I must shine in my darkest hour and that I would do nothing but praise my Father and lean into Him. My whole life prepared me for that moment. I swore I would not seek the numbing comfort of drugs, prescription or otherwise. I committed to walking through this new season with the ability to feel everything. And it hurts."

Peh's Song of Strength

God's Word isn't a set of do's and don'ts; it is the living word of life directly from His mouth. We can be women of wisdom in all we do and say. We live abundantly by every word from the mouth of God (Matthew 4:4). How can you respond with wisdom in your hard seasons? Respond like Lady Wisdom, and call out to Him even in the noisy streets and in the clamor of our lives (Proverbs 1:20). Cynthia did. "Despite this pain, God is so real to me. I believe His words and that His promises will come to fruition. I call on Him, and He is near. I understand that His ways are not my ways, and I do not expend myself on anything that is not His bread of life (Isaiah 55). Words of affirmation are valuable to me, and I recognize that I seek affirmation from people. I don't have that anymore from my husband, and the silence is deafening; it kills me. I must turn to God to affirm me. Only He can sustain me."

Strong woman, do you believe God's Word? Do you believe that when He seems silent and you scream for Him, He is there speaking volumes into your situation? Cynthia empties pen after pen as she journals, prays, and cries. She knows He is present in her pain. "I open my Bible and just read. Then I journal my thoughts and prayers. I must wait for His pursuit. I can't thank Him enough for the story He is writing in me."

Does it seem odd to be thankful for pain? When it forces us to turn to Him, we can embrace the pain. Cynthia adds, "I am in the darkest and brightest season of my life. I've needed every moment to understand the magnitude of God and His plan for me. We are so broken, but there is nothing that causes God's grace to expire. I hope my brokenness will encourage others, because it is a blessing for me to be focused on others."

Despite the pit Cynthia climbed from, she wisely uses words of encouragement and shares God's kindness, His *chesed*. She and her children spoke at her husband's memorial service. In the midst of tears and weeping, she stood and shared how thankful she was for her husband, for the man of God and father he became. "I needed to right his story. I couldn't allow one tragic moment to define the quality and character of who he was. We had a dream life. Everything everyone saw was as real as it seemed. Everything about my husband exuded God's love. It was imperative the five of us spoke the truth of who he was. We are deeply wounded by his choice, but we can stand in his honor."

As Cynthia relayed her story, I was struck by the parallels of God's love for us. He redeems our impoverished, desperate states and lavishes love over us, despite the moments our flaws threaten to define us with. And, like the love Cynthia experienced from her husband, God's love will outlive all of us. Cynthia's words are always filled with Scripture and messages that reveal her honest and raw emotions. "It is authentic to say I'm weary and broken yet again, but I am also loved by a radical redeemer. Long after I die and meet my maker, my children, friends, and family will know my love for God and for them. What we do here today continues to create our legacy throughout time. What better than to leave them with words of wisdom, kindness, and God's love and mercy? Unless we live through this, we never fully grasp the relevancy of our words. His love, His words will never end.

Peh teaches us the importance of standing face to face with God. His powerful words of creation are still spoken over you, and they say:

You are a delight.

You are loved.

You are mine.

You are more precious than jewels.

Press into Him during the pain. Even coal is pressed so the diamond within can be revealed.

We live in a broken world. We can only speak with wisdom and kindness when we experience the same from Christ. It doesn't matter what our brokenness looks like; God will fix the fractures, and His light will shine from them.

Pause and Reflect—Discussion Questions

1. Describe an opportunity you feel you spoke for God.

2. What experiences in your life can you draw from to help you speak of God's grace and loving-kindness?

3. What words of Christ give you the most comfort?

4. How can you become a woman who speaks with wisdom and kindness?

_____

_____

_____

_____

Praying the *Alef-Bet*

Lord, my desire is to delight in Your Word. Help me speak with wisdom. Confirm in my spirit when to speak and when to remain silent. Fill my heart with Your truth so it will overflow from my mouth and glorify You as a soothing balm for others. God, help me hear when You seem silent, and help me remain face to face with You. Amen.

צ or ץ

She Will Not Be Taken Captive

Tzadi—the Fish Hook, the Righteous Man

When I read this verse, I imagine a hands-on mom, immersed in her family. She anticipates every need and doesn't miss a beat. But what if she does? Is she due the honor of the Proverbs 31 Woman?

The enemy slithered in unseen and set a hook of destruction in Tara's family as her child struggled with addiction. In the process, Tara faced down shame and a taunting voice that whispered, "If only you were a better mother, this would not be happening."

Tzadi is another Hebrew letter written in two forms—straight and bent. The letter's ancient imagery is a fishhook, which symbolizes a pull toward an inescapable desire and can represent captivity. In Jewish thinking, each form represents how we approach God. Some see in the straight *tzadi* a person standing confidently with their hands raised in worship. Some see in the bent form a person kneeling in surrender or humility. Jewish commentaries relate *tzadi* to the word *tzadik*, which means a righteous person. Thus, the letter is also viewed as a symbol of righteousness and humility.

As a new mom Tara chose to leave her career that carried a sense of security and stay home to raise her children. She says, "As the prestigious paycheck left my hands, I knew God was calling me to full-time motherhood. My heart became full of the desire to see my children become future leaders for the Lord. Those early years seemed blissful. Every problem seemed solved with a nap or an early bedtime. I loved instilling the love of Jesus in their hearts. Each day ended as I tucked my children into bed and whispered my version of the priestly prayer over them, 'May the Lord bless you and keep you; may he make his face to shine on you and be gracious to you. May he rise up to meet you, and may the Lord watch over your coming and going now and forever' (Numbers 6:24–26). I'd finished with a gentle sign of the cross on their foreheads from my fingers, and I kissed them goodnight. Every day seemed filled with divine purpose. I felt like the queen of their hearts, and my little ones were mighty little men of God in my secure castle." For Tara, all was good.

Until it wasn't.

She Looks Well to the Ways of Her Household

The Hebrew word *tsaphah* opens Proverbs 31:27. It means to lean forward, peer, spy, and keep watch. *Tsaphah* is used in Psalm 5:3 when David cries, "In the morning I will order my prayer to You and eagerly watch." David leaned in, expectantly watching for God's response.

On a few occasions the NASB translates *tsaphah* as "watchman," another word reflecting the military theme of Proverbs 31. *Tsaphah* combined with *tzadi* suggests the strong woman is more than a household manager. She eagerly looks well to her home by observing, like a watchman on the wall. Satan doesn't waste time with the unfaithful; he seeks to destroy and paralyze the faithful. A watchman faithfully watches and listens. The strong woman scans the horizon, anticipating the enemy's baited hook, which threatens captivity

The Bible notes how God models *tsaphah* as He keeps watch for us.

Psalm 33:13—The Lord watches from heaven.
Psalm 66:7—His eyes watch the nations.

Psalm 127:1—He guards the city.
Proverbs 15:3—He watches the evil and the good.

How closely do you observe your family? What alerts you to look deeper? Tara faithfully surrendered to God's pull for her to leave her job and stay home full-time. What she did not anticipate was a season of captivity. "I didn't expect the teen years. The enticement of outside forces tested the strength of my calling and my children's characters. Our family went through a season of difficult losses that crippled me with fear. Two extended family members died within six months of each other and unraveled my years of godly investment. Suddenly the little hearts, once so receptive to God, were crying with unanswered questions. I had no answer but tried my best to help them cope with the grief. This was my first experience with such a devastating loss, and I didn't know how to pick up the pieces of a fractured fairy tale. I was not the strong one standing anymore. Grief caused invisible cracks in my heart and in my confidence in God's protection. Challenging influences invaded the walls of our protective fortress, especially with one child who I noticed was diving deep into substance use. I had questions too. Didn't I train and love strong enough to prevent these mistakes from happening? Was the investment I made with my whole heart a complete waste of time?"

Watchmen remain alert when the enemy breaches the wall. They know the snare is always close (Hosea 9:8). If the distracted watchman did not blow the ram's horn, the shofar, of warning and a city fell, God punished the watchman (Ezekiel 33:6). That was a heavy responsibility. I doubt God wrote the Ezekiel verse to heap guilt on mommas who mishandled the danger signals. Instead, it reminds us of the risk of stalling when the Holy Spirit prompts us of the enemy's approach. We must sound an alarm.

How do you respond when you recognize the enemy's luring hook? Not all of us face the ensuing tug of war like Tara. Our bait may be a distracting friendship or a great opportunity that realigns our focus. When the enemy gains a foothold, our focus is elsewhere. We can grow weary striving for the goodness of life. This is when we are at our weakest, and it is time to heed God's prompting. Keep watch, but God must captivate our focus.

For Tara alarm bells became routine. "As my son faced more disappointments he sank deeper into drugs, and my poor responses escalated. The equation I understood was 'bad parents equaled bad kids; good parents equaled good kids.' So I was a bad parent. Here's the real equation. All kids make mistakes, and parents don't determine their children's outcome. I purposely tried so hard to prevent problems, and yet I had to face the truth that a character breach had occurred in my son's heart."

Tara continued to embody the qualities of Proverbs 31:27. She fiercely loved her son as a raging battled ensued for his heart. She expectantly watched for God's help. "Every night I awoke feeling the presence of evil grabbing my throat, trying to restrain my voice. In response, I got out of bed and fell to my knees crying out to God for help. I refused to let my son go down without a fight. I spent hours on my face asking God to spare my son's life and rescue him from the evil influence of sin."

What helps you persist? How do you extend a lifeline to others when they are hooked? Tara felt powerless to get the needed treatment. She felt exposed to evil that tried to strangle her with shame and a sense of failure as a mom. When anxiety or the enemy stalls us, we must ask God to reveal the unknown, fine-tune our focus, and call on His power.

She Looks Well to the Ways of Her Household

These words offer another glimpse at a woman's strength. The word ways, *haliykah,* translates as "goings," "traveling company," "marching," and "caravan." *Haliykah* suggests the Proverbs woman inspects her troops as they assemble to march. The idea of a traveling company and troops indicates this watchman is not working alone. She is assembling her forces. What troops are available to you when it's time to rally?

Tara amassed forces needed to help her navigate addiction and provide financial support, counsel, and prayer. When someone we love is hooked and pulled away, we need to muster all available help. It may take a village to raise a child, but it also takes an army to defend it. For Tara, part of overcoming her debilitating oppression meant facing the rippling effects of her son's addiction head on. "Again, I fell to my knees seeking God's help in recovering my value as a mom and wife. Through seminars, support groups, and countless gifted counselors, I learned how to break from the pain of the past and the fear of the future."

Fear so often causes an emotional response instead of the logical response of leaning into God. Shame is a trap that prevents us from rallying our troops. Although Tara experienced shame's constrictive vice, she would not allow it to have the victory. Her son's life depended on it. Untangling herself from shame, she refused to believe its lie. "As mothers we are so attached to our children that we tend to own their failures. I had to understand that I could not cause, cure, or control my child's drug use. I had to hold my son accountable and responsible for his actions."

How easily can you respond like Tara? We often pray for discernment but become paralyzed when we receive it. Have you dealt with the pull of captivity in a prodigal child? Do you need a lifeline to counter the enemy's pull into shame? Please know God loves you and knows your pain. If you have never experienced this battle cry, you are blessed. But love your sisters who are in the thicket. We all need our troops to extend God's soothing grace.

Tara relates, "My son agreed to rehab. As I entrusted him into the hands of others in another state, it felt as though someone had ripped my skin off. I knew it was necessary to save my son." Isn't that the essence of redemption and restoration—to be willing to accept God's change? Even to the point of having Him rip away what we treasure most. For Tara, the path to recovery was not a straight road, and it took more time and turns than she expected. God began a good work and was going to complete it with a road that lead her son's heart home.

And Does Not Eat the Bread of Idleness

Bread, *lechem,* is most often translated as "food," and here it illustrates what the strong woman eats. "[*Lechem*] comes from a linguistic root meaning to join or connect. The modern verb 'to weld' is from the same root."[1] Think of it like this: bread holds life to the body. Here in Proverbs 31:27 the focus is not what the strong woman is serving others, but it confirms she will not feast on idleness. As Tara faced the emaciated wasteland of drug abuse she feasted on God's Word and His promises. She lost her taste for anything more. God's bread of life became her only sustenance.

Look at the word eat, *akal,* in this verse. It is sometimes translated as "devour," "burn up," "wasted," and "destroyed." This definition reveals a Hebrew wordplay with *tzadi.* The strong woman will not be hooked and devour wasteful or destructive bread. Idleness is the avoidance of activity or exertion. One commentary elaborates that the bread of idleness is a false pleasure of a lazy person, something a wise woman does not partake.[2] Tara never shrank from her responsibility. She covered her son in prayer and rallied her troops. She never indulged in the false pleasure of avoidance. Tara firmly believes her son lived because of God's grace.

---

1. Glazerson, *Building Blocks of the Soul,* 99.
2. Fox, *Proverbs 10–31,* 897.

Have you survived the enemy's attack? What verses did you feast on as you faced the famines of life that often accompany sin's captivity? I do not know the agony of drug abuse, but I do know the pain of observing someone I love navigating the hidden mines on the battlefield of depression and rebellion. I know the desperation of pleading on behalf of another with prayers that reveal my questioning heart, "God I know You *can*, but *will* You?" And, "Why *won't* You?" I know the taste of stale faith.

We are never helpless. There is a difference between idleness and being still in the presence of the Lord. As watchmen we must submit our pleas to God in trust while watching expectantly. Our job is to guard our hearts so we are not drawn into captivity. When you see forces of the enemy encircling you remember, even in your fear, to ask the Lord to open your eyes to see His provisions and protection. Unknown to Tara, as others became aware of her need, God amassed prayer warriors. He is able to send more groups and troops and provide spiritual release in ways we can never plan or imagine.

Tzadi's Song of Strength

Genesis 3:1 offers the first look at Satan's luring nature. Genesis describes him as craftier than any beast of the field. His very name is *nachash*, whose root means a whisper, a magic spell of enticement. Indeed, Satan played upon Eve's weaknesses, stringing out the line until he set his hook. He used the knowledge of good and evil as bait. When Eve desired the fruit to make her wise, she ate it (v. 6). There is imagery in the letters that spell the Hebrew word for desire, which suggest what comes from the head, our thoughts, will hook us. Eve lived in purity and perfection. She walked with God, but the power of evil slid in, fed her a lie, and she was hooked. It happens to all of us.

Temptation doesn't always mean we are lured away. Matthew 4 describes how Satan tempted Jesus in the desert. The root of the word tempt is *peira*. It means to pierce and refers to an experiment or a proving. God uses trials to test and prove our trust in Him. First Corinthians 10:13 tells us no temptation will overtake us but what is common. Our faithful God will not allow us to be tempted beyond what we are able to endure. This verse is grossly misquoted as God won't give us more than we can handle. We may face unfathomable circumstances. We cannot miss that 1 Corinthians 10:13 confirms Christ is our only escape from being overtaken.

Hebrew tradition teaches the straight *tzadi* represents one who worked to overcome the temptations of the world and willful sin through repentance. In Hebrew, this type of person is known as a *baal teshuvah*, a master of return. The bent *tzadi* is one who strives to live a godly life in complete submission to God. The straight *tzadi* stands higher than the bent because they have experienced the desire of sin but mastered the temptation. But here's the rub. We have all sinned. Our strength grows as we acknowledge the depth of our loss, repent, master our sin through the power of Christ, and return to Him.

Tara experienced the power of God's return. "Our hope that God would release our oldest child from the pull of drugs was never extinguished. As we broke out of the shame and shared our hurt and pain, many people began to pray for his return. Today, my son is free and clean of substance use and has professed a renewed faith in the power of God to set him free. My calling to be a righteous mother always comes with a struggle and a fight." The power of God through our facedown prayers pulls us back to His purpose for our lives. *Tzadi*, the fishhook, speaks metaphorically not only of forces that deceive or seduce but also of a righteous person hunted and pressed by God to bring about righteousness, faith, and endurance.

I was taught repentance means to turn from sin toward a completely different direction. Repentance encompasses more than that. The word repent, *shoov*, spelled *shin, bet* forms a powerful word picture. *Shin* is a consuming fire, and *bet* is a house. The imagery of repent means to burn down the house. We prove our trust in God when we destroy the home of our enticement and move on. We don't live in the ashes. We must shake off the ash and return to Him.

Tara's story and *tzadi* teaches us that our time of captivity does not discredit us. A strong woman never allows the enemy the victory of stealing her faith and rendering her idle. Her life reflects more than a form of godliness. She does not deny God's power. She is not captivated with the effects of sin. She is not lead away (2 Timothy 3:5–6). The strong woman stands on the wall and sounds the shofar warning, but she will not sit idle. She joins with God as He musters His army (Isaiah 13:4). She prays and wrestles to resist a captivating pull and watches eagerly as God fights for her (Joshua 23:10) and captivates her life.

Pause and Reflect—Discussion Questions

1. How would you describe the Holy Spirit's pull on your life?

_____

_____

_____

_____

2. How do you respond when you become aware of Satan's pull?

_____

_____

_____

_____

3. How would you describe idle faith?

_____

_____

_____

_____

Praying the *Alef-Bet*

Lord, I recognize my responsibility to act as a watchman over those I love. We overcome because You are greater than any captivating pull (1 John 4:4). As Your daughter, empower me to pay attention to Your wisdom and grasp the depths of Your love for me so my faith will not grow idle. In times of warning, I know You will not leave me or forsake me (1 Kings 8:57).

ק

She Is the Vital Connection

Qof—the Nape of the Neck, the Back of the Head

PROVERBS 31:28

I
f you have looked closely at the Hebrew alphabet, you might notice the letters have different spellings, meanings, and word pictures. One reason is that these differences depend on whether a letter had a pictograph meaning before the Babylonian exile. One line of thought in the development of the Hebrew script is that the ancient pictographs represented pagan gods. As the prophet Ezra reestablished worship of Israel's one true God, he changed their writing system to describe the holiness of YHWH rather than a false god. This impacts how Hebrew is viewed today. *Qof* is one of those letters with different meanings and spellings.

Fundamentally, *qof* means the back of the head near your neck. Many words containing *qof* "refer to activities of the head . . . such as spit, vomit, laugh, cry . . . and voice."[1] It represents a dome or an arch, like the arching dome of your head, which fosters the idea that it symbolizes growth cycles, or what follows. And because the Hebrew word for holy is *qodesh,* which begins with *qof,* Jewish scholars also equate the quality of holiness with the letter. For Proverbs 31:28, we will focus on the idea of the neck, what follows, and God's holiness.

---

1. Hutchens, *Hebrew for the Goyim*, 134.

Her Children Rise Up and Bless Her

We are approaching my favorite part of this rich passage: the expressions of honor bestowed on the strong woman of God. When others value our work and responsibilities, even the smallest recognition can stir up joy and help us to love even more. I think you will agree; women appreciate being appreciated. Verse 28 begins with the word *quwm*, קוּם, which means to stand up. As a reward for all she adds to her family, they stand up in her honor. It reminds me of the long-lost gesture of men standing out of respect when a woman entered a room. In some messianic congregations the men will stand and surround the women as they pray over them. It is a powerful show of respect and honor.

Julie is a Proverbs 31 Woman who was married twice to abusive men. If they stood in her presence, it was to loom over her in a threatening stance. When I asked Julie what her initial thoughts of Proverbs 31 were, she immediately recalled an incident with her first husband. "His verbal attacks were relentless, and he often spewed that passage as part of his abuse. He said I could never be such a woman. For so many women like myself, Proverbs 31 burns and leaves a mark."

Growing up, Julie attended a private Christian school, but her home life was rocky. "Starting in the second grade, one of my teachers brought me to church and continued until I was sixteen. Even though my life was riddled with abuse, I loved God, and I was saved as a little girl."

As a young adult Julie's link to Jesus was fractured. She fell into a destructive cycle and began living by her standards instead of God's. She eventually found herself as a single mother of three children and pregnant with a fourth. She chose to abort her baby. "It was a quick decision. Every fiber within me knew it was wrong, but I did it."

Can you recall a time in your life when you felt your link to Christ was severed? He promises to never leave us or forsake us. Do you believe Him? The neck is a vulnerable part of our body. If our neck is injured, we risk paralysis and the brain can't direct our body. When we sever our link to Jesus, we become desensitized to the guidance of the Holy Spirit until paralysis sets in, like what happened to Julie.

The Hebrew word for bless in this verse is *ashar*. It means a little more than just saying nice things. The blessing here is given by the Proverb woman's son. An essential lesson a son learns from his mother is how to develop his faith (2 Timothy 3:14–15). The strong woman's children stand up and bless her strength. Isn't that the hope of every mother?

Julie survived in a dark place, convinced God would never use her. "The aftermath of my abortion was incredibly difficult, but it led me back to God. As time passed, my faith strengthened even though I was alone for a long time. I was determined to date biblically. If there wasn't a man who wanted me within the boundaries of God's plan, I didn't want him." She eventually met a man who lived by the same standards. She remembered, "He was godly and treated me well. I struggled to receive his blessing because I kept waiting for the other shoe to drop. I was afraid he was too good to be true." I imagine the angels in heaven standing up and applauding as they honored God through their relationship. How easily do you receive God's blessings? Do you, like Julie, question His goodness and your worth?

Her Husband Also, and He Praises Her, Saying

The word translated as husband in this verse is *baal*, which means an owner, master, or lord. Now, before this word ruffles your feathers, remember its context. In the Ancient Near East, the husband often paid a bride price, and women were commonly viewed as property. What is radical here is that he isn't just paying her a compliment. He is praising her. The word is *halal*. It implies this man is boasting about his wife, almost like a madman. He is crazy about her. The word is also defined as to shine, give glory, and renowned. The Bible uses this word several times to indicate praise offered to the Lord. Ascribing this type of praise to a woman in the Ancient Near East was rare. The use of *baal*, or master, in this context is easier to understand when we remember Jesus as our Lord and master.

My husband does not lord over me. I don't consider him my master. My partner, yes, but not my master. He is a man of few words. When he praises me privately, my heart swells with affection for him. But when he compliments me publicly, my tightly held complaints easily dry up and blow away with the wind. Like the men of ancient Israel, his compliments are likely to be reserved for a private exchange, but they are such encouragement to me I want to bask in them.

Julie's husband is like mine. As they dated, his intentions of seeking a committed Christian woman became clear. Julie admits her history made recognizing and navigating a healthy relationship difficult. She had to be honest with him, so he had a full understanding of his choice. "I admitted my abortion. The weight and condemnation I carried was suffocating." Instead of rejection, she experienced redemption. He also had a confession. "He pulled out a piece of paper. He explained that he carried the Proverbs 31 passage in his pocket. As he got to know me, he highlighted verses that represented qualities he saw in me. He showed me the paper and told me I was the Proverbs woman, not the woman of my past. He told me I am redeemed and capable now." He encouraged her to plan the wedding of her dreams. "He wanted to celebrate me. Not the divorced woman with three kids, but me as his bride."

Pause a second. Imagine Jesus standing over you holding the Proverbs passage. He isn't checking off a list or scratching off unobtainable qualities. He's highlighting the words that describe you. He paid our bride price and sings over us, just like the husband here in Proverbs 31:28.

Qof's Song of Strength

Women are so often the connecting neck between the leadership of husbands and the family. The movie *My Big Fat Greek Wedding* has a fabulous line of dialogue that summarizes the image of *qof*. The mother is comforting her daughter Toula by explaining the husband and wife's roles. She imparts her wisdom by offering, "The man is the head, but the woman is the neck, and she can turn the head any way she wants." I doubt Toula's mother is usurping the father's leadership but instead confirming the strength of our influence. Such influence requires God's reinforcement and support.

Qof also contains the idea of a cycle, like the circuit of the sun. When we apply this understanding of *qof* to Proverbs 31:28, we see this blessing is received in due course through the cycle of the Proverb woman's life. It reminds me of the saying "What goes around comes around." As we work through the lessons of the Hebrew *alef-bet* and glean God's truth from the Proverbs 31 Woman, we will be changed, which spurs a continuous cycle of growth and of receiving God's blessing of praise. Perfect homes, perfect children, and perfect lives are not what are required to hear from our Lord and master, "Well done My good and faithful servant." It is a heart desperate for Jesus.

Julie's story continues. "My faith in God continued to strengthen, but it was so hard for me to get how much God loved me. I experienced glimpses of it through how my husband loved me. Before, the depth of God's love was just a concept. When God lifts a burden like the one I carried and you experience His blessing, all you want to do is give. I experienced amazing grace, and I wanted other women to experience it as well." Her husband encouraged her to write her story. As she did, she experienced deep healing. "I have more compassion for others who make mistakes than for myself. I was so brokenhearted for the mistakes my characters in my story made. When I realized, 'That's me!' I was freed."

There is something to be said of reviewing your brokenness. It reveals your strength. Julie looked for others to help at a crisis pregnancy center and began counseling women who were abortion-minded. She also discovered that, like her, the mothers left behind after abortion were withering away in guilt. "They may carry a perfect façade, but they need our help. My willingness to reveal my story brings healing to others. They have enough condemnation. Let's love them." Do you have experiences in your past you can draw from to help you love others? What was once intended for evil, God can use for His good. Stand up. Receive His song over you. He is blessing you. Do you know others who need to hear His song?

Pause and Reflect—Discussion Questions

1. How are you a connection between God and others?

_____

_____

_____

_____

_____

2. How is God's cycle of growth continuing in your life?

_____

_____

_____

_____

_____

3. What words do you tend to remember that have been spoken over you?

_____

_____

_____

_____

4. Is it easy or difficult for you to receive praise? Why?

_____

_____

_____

_____

Praying the *Alef-Bet*

Lord, I release my burdens in life and stand up to praise You. I receive this song of strength You sing over me. Help me to hold my head high because Your love supports and sustains me always. Amen.

ר

She Places God First

Resh—the Head, First in Rank

PROVERBS 31:29

Surely Proverbs 31:29 is to encourage only those women who have followed the biblical model of marriage, submission, and womanhood. And those who, when it comes to following Christ, have crossed all the t's and dotted all the i's, whose work for God excels anything I might offer in comparison. They deserve the accolades. But the Word of God doesn't only apply to a select few, does it? His promises and compliments are for me, for you, and for women who are forced to adapt man's traditional expectations of a godly marriage to fit their reality. Women like Jennifer, who you will meet in this chapter.

Proverbs 31:29 is the continuation of verse 28. They relate words of praise the husband proclaims over his wife. *Resh* is the Aramaic word for head, which is the letter's word picture. It relates to the most important, like a head of state, a ruler, and preeminent. From its idea of being first in line it also represents the beginnings of a cycle.

This verse is commonly used to praise the wife who has brought honor to her husband. Especially so in the traditional Christian home where the husband is honored as the spiritual leader and the wife lovingly submits to his leadership. This is the dream we are sold. But what if we are dealing with a single woman or single mother? What if the husband is not able to fulfill his traditional role physically or spiritually? Where do you fit in these descriptions? Does this disqualify you or these women from receiving this praise?

Man Daughters Have Done Nobly

The memory trigger for Proverbs 31:29 is the Hebrew word for many. *Resh* indicates this woman has priority. She is first over many. The word for women here is actually the Hebrew word for daughters and implies that this rare, worthy-of-pursuit woman "went forth from [her father's house] and brought credit to it."[1]

Her father is honored, God acknowledges her value, and now her husband makes the same acknowledgment. She is indeed a noble woman. The same word for noble was used in verse 10 to start this poem. It is the word *chayil*. This passage is structured as a chiastic poem, meaning the beginning and ending passage parallel each other. Her husband acknowledges her strength as a yoked partner, and here he rises to acknowledge her strength again.

Jennifer took a chance dating someone she knew was soon leaving for boot camp. "He was physically fit, loved being outdoors, and confident. These were his qualities I first fell in love with."

They both had a background of faith. After they married, they knew the importance of finding a good church and committed their marriage to putting Christ first. This desire was solidified as they expected their first child and grasped the responsibility of raising their children in a Christian home. Her husband relished in leading his family and was instrumental in finding the church their family would call home.

Within months after their first child was born, Jennifer's appendix ruptured. Complications resulted in a lengthy, debilitating recovery. When she looks back on that time, she recognizes the hand of God

---

1. Fox, *Proverbs 10–31*, 898.

as her husband cared for her. Her healing included a quieting of her spirit as she submitted to her husband's leadership and the teachings the church poured into her. "My husband was my rock and played a huge part in nurturing my body and my faith. It was during this time I rededicated myself to Christ. Even though I had a background in the church, I had to rethink my role as a wife and mother." She gladly submitted to the wife's traditional role under her husband's leadership and valued his support and praise.

But You Excel Them All

Proverbs 31:29 offers an additional parallel to the strength of this woman. The husband acknowledges the sacrifice of this strong woman. He tells her, "You excel them all." The word excel is *alah,* and it primarily means to go up or to ascend. It can also be translated as superior or first, and this is the link to *resh.*

Alah shares a Hebrew root with the word *olah,* which also means to go up, to ascend. But *olah* relates to burnt offerings and sacrifice and is associated with the way in which the smoke from a sacrificial offering ascends as a fragrance before God. This offering differs from others. Where other offerings may be portioned to the priests, this burnt offering is entirely consumed and goes up in flames on the altar to God in worship. This gives us a clue to some wordplay with the link to sacrifice. Not only is the woman of Proverbs 31 strong and a servant to others, like *alef* the ox, but she is also acknowledged for the sacrifices she makes. Isn't acknowledgment what we all desire? I'm willing to sacrifice for my family, and I do whatever it takes. I do so knowing my sacrifice may go unnoticed. To have my husband or children acknowledge my sacrifice is high praise indeed.

Jennifer's husband was in the United States Navy intelligence agency, which required him to serve in the war-torn regions of Afghanistan and Iraq. In the first nine years of their marriage, he spent much of it with his boots on the ground in perilous situations. When he finally returned home, he carried both physical and mental injuries. He was a man Jennifer barely recognized.

His injuries required Jennifer to reverse their roles, and she became his primary caretaker and the family's breadwinner. Gone were her expectations of the family she hoped for. "I planned to do better with my family. I wanted my kids to have it better than I ever did in a traditional family, with the traditional structure of a strong father leading them. I thought our family would be perfect and easy because my husband and I worked together to achieve that ideal." As her husband struggled in acclimating to his life at home, Jennifer faced her new normal. "We moved into survival mode. I had to accept that God was molding us into His plan, not my standards."

She confronted the fact that she had to sacrifice the scripted life she dreamed of. "I wanted to homeschool and go back to college, but it fell on me to become the leader of our family. Even my career realigned because I had to put everyone else first. My husband's injuries impacted his motivation. Depression hangs over him like a thick black cloud. I saved his life once, when I walked in on his attempt to take his life."

When we hold up Pinterest and airbrushed advertising against a harsh reality, it is easy to view our worth, with these standards, as a failure. Women, especially wives and mothers, seek validation and credibility from their family. Every woman is different. Some women work, homeschool, and have strong husbands who lead. For others, leading is their responsibility. Do you compare yourself with the world's standards? So many of us do. Like apples to oranges, it isn't a fair comparison.

Proverbs begins with a statement that sets its theme: "The fear of the Lord is the beginning of knowledge" (Proverbs 1:7). The book then details the lessons, warnings, and the importance of wisdom. The theme is finalized in Proverbs 31 as encouragement for us to be strong women, whose foremost priority (*resh*), is to understand that the beginning of wisdom is to fear God. As she excels, her husband, or bridegroom, stands and acknowledges her worth and sacrifices. The last detail he admires is her priority of yoking herself to God and drawing wisdom from Him. Her last-mentioned quality points back to the first, most important quality of Proverbs.

A full cycle.

This cycle reminds me of a phrase repeated throughout the Old Testament. When the lives of kings were recorded, the scribes often added the words, "Now the rest of his acts and all his ways, from first to last, behold, they are written in the Book of the Kings of Judah and Israel" (2 Chronicles 28:26; see also 35:27). This is a way to state that all the deeds of the king, from A–Z, have been recorded. It's interesting that Proverbs, known as the Book of Wisdom, ends with a similar tribute. The phrase from first to last is echoed in Matthew 20:16, which records Jesus saying something similar, "So the last shall be first, and the first last." This is an old Semitic idiom meaning "in this we are equal."

These final verses of Proverbs are a nod to the strong woman's characteristics and her embodiment of wisdom from A–Z. It is praise from a loving, heavenly Bridegroom who desires to remind His bride that when we stand before the throne of God, there is no hierarchy of roles. All of our deeds, our works of service, our teaching, and expressions of love, from A–Z, will be displayed before him on a level playing field. Our service will not be compared to Mother Teresa or Corrie ten Boom or the super Christian we have placed on a pedestal as more worthy. When it comes to the work in God's kingdom, we are all yoked to Jesus, we draw on His strength, and He equally supports all.

Resh's Song of Strength

Jennifer is not only her family's primary caretaker and breadwinner, but she is also the force that seeks and applies for veteran's assistance and services that provide needed family excursions, surgeries, and therapies for her husband's recovery. More than once she has wanted to quit, leave their marriage, and let her husband fend for himself. Feelings of defeat and failure accompanied each offer of help, and accepting the help was difficult. I can relate. Somehow accepting help prompts condemnation of weakness. How do you receive help when you walk through hard times? For Jennifer, "The stress carried me to a point of daily panic attacks, and the depression overwhelmed me as well. I had my own health issues, and I didn't even want to get out of bed either." God was gentle, and he used her most vulnerable time to give her a glimpse of her husband's daily struggle. "God filled me with such compassion for my husband. I couldn't leave. I knew God was working on me, maybe more so my husband. I had to heal and care for myself if we were going to survive. I also began to understand how others feel when I don't accept their help. It blocks their blessing."

So how can a woman like Jennifer emulate the Proverbs 31 Woman? She is one who sincerely desired to follow the Christian framework with her husband leading their family, but their life is a complete contrast. Because of her husband's injuries, she is their leader physically, mentally, and spiritually, yet she still honors her husband by putting Christ first. The process has been slow and arduous at times. The difference now is that she relies on the Holy Spirit daily to make it through. Jennifer adds, "I'm stubborn. I just won't stop." She laughed at her acknowledgment, "That can be both good and bad." She also prays constantly. "My husband is not able to talk through some of the conflicts I face, so I pour my heart out to God, and I'm in His Word daily. I've learned to fall into the rhythm of my husband's leading. I still do the research and the work, but I wait for his approval and for him to agree before making a final decision. Sometimes I still must push him, and we argue, but we have a tempo."

What is the pulse of your life? Your life, goals, and accomplishments may take several turns away from your original plan, but you still rise above like a fragrant offering before God. You are so important to

Him. He desires that others recognize your strength and sacrifice. Many daughters are strong, but you excel them all. What would it take in your life to believe that?

Jennifer continues to recognize the hand of God, and He has always come through. "For a while, I was very angry at God, but now I see how I've grown through the struggle and challenges. I'm not thankful we are hurting, or for what my husband experienced, but I am thankful for the growth. I listen for God's leadership. I know He is speaking when I feel that deep ache in my soul. I always spend time in prayer and God's Word for confirmation, but I know God speaks." Her husband is healing. "His moods are more pleasant. He sleeps better. He was blessed with a service dog, and she has made all the difference. He is now more likely to go out with us. This season is incredibly hard, but through all of this, I am stronger."

Strong is another word we tend to put in the same category as perfection or courageous. It's all or nothing. We are told that in the processes of survival, we must be perfect, courageous, and strong. But perfect is reaching the point of completion. Courage is acknowledging your fears and weaknesses and doing the task anyway. Strong may be just getting out of bed in the morning. It is in those days that we need to reach deep inside and grasp God's promise of Psalm 118:14, "The LORD is my strength and song, and He has become my salvation."

I've heard people say, "I never pray for patience because God will send opportunities to test my patience time and time again." I think this applies to everything we pray for. God will test us through our weakness. He must, after all, to strengthen that area. After a good workout, the muscles we used are the ones that hurt the next day. The use brings pain, but the pain brings strength.

A full cycle.

Pause and Reflect—Discussion Questions

1. Think through your responsibilities in life and prioritize your top five. Who or what have you placed as number one?

_____

_____

_____

_____

_____

2. How easily do you place your needs before your family's? Do you recognize areas where, if you prioritized them higher, you would be in better physical, mental, or spiritual health?

_____

_____

_____

_____

_____

3. How easily do you recognize when you need help? How easily do you accept help from others?

_____

_____

_____

_____

_____

4. How can placing Christ first in your life help you to better honor
   other authorities in your life?

_____

_____

_____

_____

_____

Praying the *Alef-Bet*

Lord, I have placed You as preeminent in my life. All I have and all I
have accomplished is because You are first. I have honored You, and
here in Proverbs, I receive Your acknowledgment and honor. Thank
You, Father. Amen.

She Is Praised

Shin—the Teeth, Fire, to Destroy

PROVERBS 31:30

L inda met her husband right out of high school. His buzz cut and tattoos were a stark contrast from the other young men in the decade of long hair and bell-bottoms, and the least likely person to attract Linda's interest. Theirs was a whirlwind romance. They met in November, were engaged in December, and married in February. Although both were firmly rooted in their church and a faith in Jesus, they would face a life of testing, refining, and repentance.

Shin is another letter of contrasts. It is a letter included in the spellings of the Hebrew words for crush and peace, sin and repent. It has two forms and two names, *sin* and *shin*. Both forms carry the primary word picture of teeth and the secondary of ideas of fire and passion.

Healthy teeth are strong and firmly rooted while rotting teeth can signal illness. Like teeth, fire can consume and destroy. In contrast, it can also refine and be an agent of transformational change. This refining process of fire is often linked as a symbol for God and His divine power and passion for us. Jews believe the letter *shin* represents two names of God, *El Shaddai*, the all-sufficient God, and the God of *Shalom*, unlimited peace. Drawing from the all-sufficient God of peace would become a consuming theme for Linda and her husband.

Charm Is Deceitful and Beauty Is Vain

This verse begins with the Hebrew word *sheqer*. It means a lie, a sham, and deceit. It's a strong word. The pictographs that form this word contain images revealing destruction at the back of a head. Lies are shams often spread behind the back of their target. Have you experienced the destructive nature of *sheqer*? There is a Chinese proverb that says, "A lie has no legs and cannot stand, but it has wings and can fly far and wide." Few things destroy like deceit.

A few years into their marriage, employment moved Linda and her husband far from family, but Linda occasionally returned for visits. During one visit, her grandmother became sick, and it required her to stay longer than usual. Despite several reassuring phone calls with her husband, Linda sensed something was not right. A heaviness descended over her, one she just couldn't shake. When she finally returned home to her husband, he revealed the dreaded news of his encounter with a coworker, which had grown into a relationship. When she asked if he was willing to stop, he said no. "It completely took my breath away. I wanted to know how he could do this as a believer, as my husband, and why? I couldn't believe his response and lack of remorse. Some suggested he was not really saved. But I had no doubt our marriage was built on Christ, and it wasn't a sham."

Satan, as the father of lies, seeks to kill, steal, and destroy (John 10:10). "Many encouraged me to leave my husband and told me I was stupid for staying. I knew God knit us together, and I chose to stay with my husband." Linda sought her pastor's council. Once the pastor understood she had no desire to leave her husband, he said, "You want it to work? So now you fight." Linda girded herself with the strength of God's Word and engaged her husband's actions and attitudes with prayer. How do you respond to destructive behavior? Do you tend to fight or do you resort to flight? Linda approached her husband with grace; she did not degrade, accuse, or attack. "I fell into God daily. It was the hardest battle I have ever faced."

Sheqer describes charm as a sham. The Hebrew word for charm in this verse is *chen*, which means graciousness, grace or favor. Not the perfect, continuous grace of Christ but the favor people share and retract depending on our mood and other's behavior. The word acknowledges the human limitations of the Proverbs woman. Like her beauty, which is described as a breath or vapor, the grace, favor, or acceptance she extends to others, if based on her strength, has the potential to be a sham and will disappear quickly.

Linda needed all of God's grace and peace she could muster. For weeks she watched the other woman deposit her husband at home many evenings after work. Some nights he didn't return. How do you draw on God's peace amid a raging war? Linda was on the attack. She anointed her husband's side of the bed and fervently prayed. One evening she boldly confronted her husband and claimed the blood of Jesus over the spirit influencing him. She was weary from battle, and the depth of her pain seemed limitless. She held firm during the lowest points, found God's peace, and returned to the battle for her husband.

Commentators suggest the husband's description of the Proverbs 31 Woman ends with verse 29. Verses 30 and 31 return to the scribe's point of view. The wording suggests the woman's physical beauty has faded, and if her husband or children were saying this, it would not be very complimentary. I agree. Most women would not be pleased if their husband were to proclaim, "My wife's grace and beauty are a sham!" I'm laughing a little just thinking about it.

These final verses are a moral lesson for the reader. They warn against attributing a woman's value based on her beauty. Instead, her value is found in her fear of the Lord. A lesson Linda's husband was slow to learn. What in your life is worth fighting for? How can you endure if the Lord calls you into battle? The effects of her husband's affair took a toll on Linda. She was plagued by nightmares. As she cried in silence and buried her feelings, she questioned the value of her marriage.

God's timing is sovereign. As Linda pretended to sleep, her husband crept in late the very night she packed her bags and planned to leave. He quietly knelt next to the bed and embraced her. "Can you forgive me?" he pleaded. "I don't know why I did this or why this happened. God has been relentless. I've been fighting with Him for days, screaming at Him to leave me alone and get off my back!" At an earlier meeting that day, as her husband met with the other woman, he affirmed his love for his wife. He wanted to spend his life with Linda. Incredibly, he even shared with the woman how he came to believe in Jesus and God's power in his life.

God heard every one of Linda's prayers, caught every tear, and knew her breaking point. "We slowly started putting things back together, but we just didn't talk about it and instead acted as though nothing happened. I realize now that was a mistake. We should have talked. Before the affair, I was friendly, social, and gracious. I grew up in an environment of encouragement. After the affair, I was insecure. I felt dismissed and unattractive. I constantly found my flaws despite my husband's reassurance that I wasn't to blame." The affair scarred Linda's heart, but her marriage survived. "I look back and realize that leaving would have forfeited God's healing, and Satan would have won."

What experiences have you faced that changed how you view yourself or removed your confidence? Listening to Satan's lies is easy. They so often drown out God's whispers of love and His passion for us.

But a Woman Who Fears the LORD, She Shall Be Praised

It's important to understand this word fear. Although it can be translated as an unpleasant emotion like dread or terror, here it is used more as respect or reverence of God. The Hebrew word is *yare*. To *yare*, fear,

God, means you respect and value God so much you fear wounding or breaking His heart. When we live like this, God reveals Himself to us to know, *yada*, Him on a deeper level. As our intimate knowledge of Him grows so does His value.

The Proverbs woman's fear of the Lord is praised more than her housekeeping skills and financial gains. Even her extension of grace and loving-kindness are only a fleeting vapor when compared to her devotion and fear of the Lord. If you were to rank your reverence of God, with one being the lowest to five being the highest, how would you score? Like me, it likely changes daily, but imagine how different our lives could be if we filtered our every action through our respect and reverence for God. That is a Proverbs 31 Woman in action.

Shin's Song of Strength

We must pause to honor the Jewish perspective of the Proverbs 31 passage as it relates it to wisdom and instruction. When Jewish men recite their morning prayer, they wrap a leather strap attached to tefillin, little black boxes holding portions of the Torah, around their head and their arm. This is done to symbolically bind and align their head, heart, and hands with the heart of God. The tefillin are engraved with a *shin*, a symbol for God.

Even though Jewish women are forbidden from wearing tefillin, they do not shirk the importance of reading and memorizing God's wisdom. As we become more intimate with God, we align our hearts with His. He pours into us a spirit of wisdom so we will know the purpose of our calling, which is to honor Him first, above all else (Ephesians 1:17–18). This is the calling of all believers. This is the beginning of wisdom and the origins of God's refining fire.

Fire is used to smelt gold, silver, and other metals. It burns away any foreign elements and transforms the metal into the purest ore. Applying this imagery to the Proverbs 31 Woman helps us recognize the importance of having a spirit willing to be refined and transformed. As God burns away the impurities in our hearts, He reveals the purest essence of His love for us.

Decades after the affair, Linda discovered she was to stand toe to toe in battle again. "My husband received a Facebook message that read, 'I feel that God has laid on my heart to send you this message. If you'd like to connect, feel free to message me. If not, I understand; no hard feelings either way.'" Unknown to them, the affair created a child. "We were completely shocked. We never knew about her. Getting a message like that thirty-seven years later will turn your whole world upside down. Suddenly, every emotion of fear, doubt, and worthlessness came rushing back." But this time, she and her husband were unshakable. They remained firmly rooted in Christ, like the healthy strong teeth of *shin,* as God's refining fires blew over them again.

"I questioned God so many times, 'How do I deal with this? Now?' God always answered that I was to accept her with a mother's heart. She, her husband, and their children are fully embraced. They are a part of us. To them, we are Daddy, Mom, Grammy, and Grampy." The grace each woman extended to the other was the healing balm needed to restore years of Satan's lies. "I forgave the other woman years ago, and through God's grace we are able to share this beautiful family. Through it all, God reminded me what the enemy meant for evil and harm, God has made good" (Genesis 50:20). The memory trigger may be that this woman, who fears God, is firmly planted in her faith and not one rooted in decay who vainly portrays a fleeting outward façade. Do you think you could have extended grace as Linda did? At the time, she never thought it possible, but today she reaps His great reward.

There is another bit of wordplay in this verse. Proverbs 31:30 duplicates the praise she receives from her husband in Proverbs 31:28. Both verses use the word *halal* for praise. We learned this word means to celebrate and to shine, a root for the word hallelujah. In some cases, *halal* is also used to describe the adverse actions of boasting or making a fool of someone. If *shin*, a letter of contrasts, is used to trigger memorization, perhaps the reader is to remember the contrasts of being a transforming fire versus a fire of destruction. Or the contrast of sharp biting teeth or teeth chewing over truth. Or the *halal* of praise versus the *halal* of foolish boasting. Where do you fall on the spectrum? When we are women of strength who rightly fear God, we are worthy of praise. Thank You, Jesus!

God is in the business of restoration. He makes up for the years lost to the locust (Joel 2:25). Linda and her husband founded a ministry that provides clothing and shoes to children who have been victims of abuse or neglect and are removed suddenly from their home without their basic requirements. Their goal is to aid foster families, grandparents, or other family members who are called unexpectedly to take in a child. Part of her job requires her to stand before hundreds and share how her family is the prime example of God's refining fire and grace. "On my own, I wouldn't have the grace to forgive or accept God's complete restoration. The cloud of hurt, insecurity, and anger over my heart has been wrung out and lifted. I am a lot stronger than I ever imagined."

Shin suggests a final contrast between the wisdom of fearing God versus the vanity and wisdom of the world, which will ultimately disappear. By the world's standard, Linda and her husband should have never survived. The strong woman of Proverbs 31 is clearly a contrast from the typical women of her time. Proverbs 31:30 empowers us to understand our value is not contained in beauty. The one who will receive from the Lord, "Well done, good and faithful slave" (Matthew 25:21) when it really matters is the woman who fears the Lord. Do you need to hear the song God sings over you? Your physical beauty is but a breath. It is YHWH who is eternal, and He will shine upon you and boast in you as a woman who seeks and reveres Him. These are your qualities of timeless beauty. Beloved, He sings this heroic hymn for you.

Pause and Reflect—Discussion Questions

1. How would you define fear of the Lord? How is it evident in your life?

_____

_____

_____

_____

_____

2. Are there any impurities in your life requiring God's refining? How accepting are you of His refinement?

_____

_____

_____

_____

_____

3. Our beauty is so much more than our fleeting physical appearance. What eternal beauty has God bestowed you? Ashes may be a result of destruction, mourning, and withering faith, but He trades beauty for ashes (Isaiah 61:3). What image do you need to trade for His beauty?

_____

_____

_____

_____

_____

Praying the *Alef-Bet*

Lord, You are the God of peace, and Your passion for me is relentless. God, I pray You are always before me as a reminder of Your constant refinement in my life. Fan the flame of my faith and reverence for You so it will remain firmly planted and not fade like a vapor. Amen.

She Leaves a Legacy

Tav—the Cross, the Mark

We've reached the final letter of the Hebrew alphabet. *Tav's* word picture is a cross. It relates to making a mark, like a signature or leaving a sign, like X marks the spot. It is difficult to look at a cross without considering its symbolism of Christ's crucifixion. It's interesting to note the cross was a symbol of reverence and spirituality in several civilizations thousands of years before His death. When we see a sign or a marking, we expect to believe what it represents. Road signs warn us of falling rocks, animal crossings, and lanes merging, and we think this to be true. Because of this, *tav* has developed into a symbol of truth.

Marks of identification are common in the Bible. The first biblical use of the word *sign* is in Genesis 1:14, when God hung the lights of the sky to be a sign for seasons, days, and years and to mark boundaries of time. Others are noted.

Genesis 17:11 and Exodus 13:9, 16—These verses mention the mark of consecration of the first born as a recognition of the covenant relationship with God.

211

Exodus 12:7—The Israelites marked their door with the blood of
the Passover lamb to protect them from the angel of death,
God's final curse against Pharaoh.

Ezekiel 9:4—The foreheads of those who groaned over sin were
marked and spared God's judgment.

Revelation 7:1–8; 22:4—God's name will mark the foreheads of
His bondservants.

Baptism is considered an outward sign of a Christian's commitment to
Christ (Colossians 2:11–12), as is our love for one another (John 13:35).
Throughout history, God has identified those who are His with a mark,
His *tav* of covenant and protection.

It is fascinating the last letter of the *alef-bet* is a symbol of truth.
For me, it spurs an awareness that God's Word, from A–Z, ends and
is sealed with truth. The Hebrew word for truth is *amet*, spelled *alef,
mem, tav*. If we were to write the Hebrew *alef-bet* and include all forms
of the letters, it would contain twenty-seven letters. *Alef* would be first.
Mem would land right in the middle. And *tav* would be the final letter.
The strategic placement of these letters reveals God's truth and is fully
contained in the *alef-bet*. Incredible.

The earliest form of a signature was to make some type of mark
of ownership. Even today, some will sign their names with an X.
This is *tav*. Did you know God signed His masterpiece of creation?
Genesis 2:3 reveals a divine word and letter play. It describes God's
final actions of creation, "Then God blessed the seventh day and sanc-
tified it, because in it He rested from all His work which God had
created and made."

The last three words of this verse in Hebrew read, from right to left
בָּרָא אֱלֹהִים לַעֲשׂוֹת.

You might recognize the final letters of each word—*alef, mem,
tav*—truth. God breathed out and spoke all of creation, and the last
phrase bestowing the completion of creation encompasses truth.

This certainly gives us a new understanding of Psalm 119:160, "The sum of Your word is truth." But God didn't stop there. You see, the final letter, on the final word, describing the final day of creation, is a *tav*. God added the final hue of color then signed His name across creation to mark His ownership over all. The Bible never ceases to amaze.

Strong woman, God finishes the final verse of this hymn for you. It is as though He is singing, "Beloved, you have remained strong and steadfast. Your works deserve recognition. I acknowledge and validate all you do at your door, the city gate, and beyond."

Give Her the Product of Her Hands

The memory trigger for Proverbs 31:31 means to give, put upon, appoint, or designate. The final legacy of this woman will be to ascribe to her the value of her accomplishments. She works in service to provide for her family. She teaches and guides. She rolls up her sleeves, takes up her sword, and stands diligently as a watchman while surrendering to God in a life set apart for Him. A final stanza of praise is now sung over her in celebration of the fruit, the work of her hand. By the way, hand in this verse is *yad* not *kaf*. It references her strength, and ownership.

There was a time when work in the home was labor intensive for basic survival. The task of boiling water included walking to draw water, carrying it back, collecting firewood, building a fire, hefting the water over the fire, and the often-perilous task of removing the boiling water for use. Women of biblical time deserved praise for being strong enough to survive. Today we turn a knob, flip a switch, and place a pot. We navigate the dangers of disgruntled bosses and treacherous commutes. Or perhaps we survive the landmines of moody teenagers, vindictive exes, and foul tongues. We overcome the death toll of depression, poverty, and abuse. Regardless, God uses this heroic hymn as a way of acknowledging your survival and the work you are doing both physically and spiritually.

And Let Her Works Praise Her in the Gates

God chooses a thought-provoking place to acknowledge the Proverbs 31 Woman. Some translations note it as the door to her house. Others say the city gates. Both are important locations. When God acknowledges our work at home, He confirms its value. Many women don't receive this type of validation or credit. For the stay-at-home wife or the homeschooling mama, the work you do is important. For the juggling working mother in the trenches at the city gate, the work you do is important. For the single or childless woman , the work you do is important. Ladies, we balance so many roles, and we work tirelessly. Hear this from me, the sisterhood, and the God you love: praise your work.

God uses *hallel* for the third time in this passage. The Proverbs woman's husband praised her in verse 28. Her fear and reverence of the Lord evokes praise in verse 30. And now, her lasting mark on the world, her legacy, is praised. Do you remember the significance of the number three? It stands for what is full and substantial. Three signifies a mark of completion. I don't believe there are coincidences with God or His Word. We are encountering the final verse in a passage that details the strength of women. It is here God inspired a scribe to offer a third and final mark of His praise. Please don't miss that we are experiencing God's fullness in a passage about women.

God marks His Word with incredible stories of strong women. Esther, Tamara, Rahab, Abigail, Hannah, Deborah, and Ruth come to mind. Some sources order the books of the Tanakh, the Hebrew Bible, with Ruth following Proverbs. What better way to finish a teaching on wisdom and the strength of a woman than to flesh it out in Naomi and Ruth? Boaz calls Ruth a woman of excellence, *chayill* (Ruth 3:11). The

Book of Ruth is a story of two women whose combined ages span a lifetime. Our legacy unfolds throughout our lives, and it will be praised at the end. Ruth and Naomi faced crippling losses and overcame mounting adversities, just like the women whose stories you encountered in this book.

The final words praising Ruth are proclaimed over her at the city gates (Ruth 4:15). But the Book of Ruth is about Naomi too, who had suffered and lost more than Ruth. Her legacy is also revealed at the city gates as she held the long hoped-for seed of our Redeemer on her lap. Naomi, whose name means pleasant, renamed herself bitter and embraced the bitterness of her life. Yet she was redeemed in the women's accolades at the city gates. Years later, Mary, another woman whose name means bitter, watched as her son Jesus was crucified outside of the city gates on a Cross so we could experience God's good pleasure (Hebrews 13:12). Jesus shed those round red drops of treasured blood to mark us as His.

What legacy do you want to leave? Do you want others to remember you were a good cook? An organized planner? Someone who was smart, beautiful, helpful, loving? These are all worthy legacies but not our ultimate goal in Christ. Are you on the correct path for leaving a legacy that reflects Christ? Or do you feel your reputation and failures exceed any positive mark you can leave on this world and cross-out any hope of being a Proverbs 31 Woman? You are in good company. One aspect of the Bible I cling to is the theme of God using the unusable. He uses people, not despite their inadequacies but because of them.

Rahab, the harlot, is listed in the lineage of Jesus.
Joseph, the youngest, didn't realize bragging about his dreams would fan the flames of jealousy in his brothers. He was thrown into a pit and sold into slavery, only to be used to save God's chosen people.

David, the least likely, was a murdering adulterer drowning in
parental failures but still called a man after God's own heart.
Tamar, the widow, was used by her father-in-law then cast aside
only to become a lioness in the lineage of the tribe of Judah.
Paul, a murdering, legalistic Rabbi, surrendered to the goads of
Christ to reach the very group he prosecuted.

There are so many more, Abraham and Ruth, the foreign-born pagans,
Isaac and Jacob, the second-born sons, Leah, who was loved less, and
Nebuchadnezzar, a godless, thieving lunatic who ultimately exalted and
praised the Most High God.

The people of the Bible were real, with real struggles and failures. Just
like us. But look at God's legacy of truth revealed through their lives.

We too survive:

Adultery
Promiscuity
Jealousy
Parental Fails
Abuse and Rejection
Legalism

But God has left His mark on you.

We are fearfully and wonderfully part of His creation. God, through
His Son Jesus Christ, left His final signature of provision on you. By the
marks slashed across His body, we are healed (1 Peter 2:24).

The legacy of the women in this book are not signs of those trying to claw through or escape the pits of defeat and shame. Instead,
they are signatures on marriage licenses, new homes, adoption papers,
love letters, and books. Their marks reflect the truth of God's love and
redemption. His fingerprints are revealed as He shapes them into
women of strength, worthy of this heroic song.

Life is grueling, but God is greater. You are not disqualified. Put Him first. Love Him with all your heart, soul, and mind. He has an incredible legacy of strength for you. Allow Christ to complete this work in you so your legacy will bring honor to your Bridegroom, the love of your life, Jesus Christ. The legacy I desire to leave is to be known as *eshet chayill—strong woman*. Through Christ, it can be yours as well.

Pause and Reflect—Discussion Questions

1. What legacy would you like to leave?

_____

_____

_____

_____

_____

_____

2. How are you making this legacy happen in your life?

_____

_____

_____

_____

_____

_____

Praying the *Alef-Bet*

Lord, You are the author and perfecter of our faith. I pray my legacy includes the words from Your mouth, "Well done, good and faithful servant" (Matthew 25:21 NIV). Lord, Your mark on me is the only mark I want to leave on this world. Amen.

**If you enjoyed this book, will you consider sharing
the message with others?**

Let us know your thoughts at info@ironstreammedia.com.
You can also let the author know by visiting or sharing a photo
of the cover on our social media pages or leaving a review
at a retailer's site. All of it helps us get the message out!

Facebook.com/IronStreamMedia

Ascender Books, New Hope® Publishers, Iron Stream Books,
and New Hope Kidz are imprints of Iron Stream Media,
which derives its name from Proverbs 27:17,
"As iron sharpens iron, so one person sharpens another."

This sharpening describes the process of discipleship,
one to another. With this in mind, Iron Stream Media provides
a variety of solutions for churches, ministry leaders, and nonprofits ranging
from in-depth Bible study curriculum and Christian book publishing
to custom publishing and consultative services. Through our popular
Life Bible Study, Student Life Bible Study brands, and New Hope imprints,
ISM provides web-based full-year and short-term Bible study teaching
plans as well as printed devotionals, Bibles, and discipleship curriculum.

For more information on ISM and Ascender Books, please visit

IronStreamMedia.com

If you enjoyed *Strength of a Woman*,
you will also enjoy:

You may also enjoy:

Available from NewHopePublishers.com
or your favorite retailer.